Fortress of the Muslim

PROPHETIC INVOCATIONS
FROM THE QURAN & SUNNAH

Fortress of the Muslim

PROPHETIC INVOCATIONS
FROM THE QURAN & SUNNAH

Sa'id bin Ali bin Wahf Al-Qahtani

1 2 3 4 5 6 7 8 9 10

All rights reserved. No part of this publication may be reproduced, stored in a retrieval system or transmitted in any form or by any means – electronic, mechanical, photocopying, recording or otherwise – without written permission from the publisher.

© Light Publishing 2014

Sa'id bin Ali bin Wahf Al-Qahtani

Fortress of the Muslim
Prophetic invocations from the
Quran and Sunnah

ISBN 978-1-915570-00-0

www.lightpublishing.co.uk

بسم الله الرحمن الرحيم

CONTENTS

1. When waking up — 15
2. Supplication when wearing a garment — 17
3. Supplication said when wearing a new garment — 17
4. Supplication said to someone wearing a new garment — 18
5. Before undressing — 18
6. Before entering the toilet — 19
7. After leaving the toilet — 19
8. When starting ablution — 19
9. Upon completing the ablution — 20
10. When leaving the home — 21
11. Upon entering the home — 22
12. Supplication when going to the mosque — 22
13. Upon entering the mosque — 23
14. Upon leaving the mosque — 23
15. Supplications related to the adhan (the call to prayer) — 24
16. Supplication at the start of the prayer (after takbir) — 26
17. While bowing in prayer (ruku') — 33

18.	Upon rising from the bowing position	35
19.	Supplication whilst prostrating (sujud)	36
20.	Supplication between the two prostrations	38
21.	Supplication when prostrating due to recitation of the Quran	39
22.	The Tashahud	40
23.	Prayers upon the Prophet ﷺ after the tashahud	41
24.	Supplication said after the last tashahud and before salam	43
25.	Remembrance after salam	50
26.	Supplication for seeking guidance in forming a decision or choosing the proper course…etc (al-Istikharah)	55
27.	Remembrance said in the morning and evening	57
28.	Remembrance before sleeping	69
29.	Supplication when turning over during the night	77
30.	Upon experiencing unrest, fear, apprehensiveness and the like during sleep	78
31.	Upon seeing a good dream or a bad dream	78
32.	Qunut al-Witr	79
33.	Remembrance immediately after salam of the witr prayer	82

34.	Supplication for anxiety and sorrow	83
35.	Supplication for one in distress	84
36.	Upon encountering an enemy or those of authority	86
37.	Supplication for one afflicted with doubt in his faith	87
38.	Settling a debt	88
39.	Supplication for one afflicted by whisperings in prayer or recitation	89
40.	Supplication for one whose affairs have become difficult	89
41.	Upon committing a sin	90
42.	Supplication for expelling the devil and his whisperings	90
43.	Supplication when stricken with a mishap or overtaken by an affair	91
44.	Placing children under Allah's protection	
45.	When visiting the sick	92
46.	Excellence of visiting the sick	93
47.	Supplication of the sick who have renounced all hope of life	94
48.	Instruction for the one nearing death	95
49.	Supplication for one afflicted by a calamity	95
50.	When closing the eyes of the deceased	96
51.	Supplication for the deceased at the	

	funeral prayer	97
52.	Supplication for the advancement of reward during the funeral prayer	100
53.	Condolence	101
54.	Placing the deceased in the grave	102
55.	After burying the deceased	102
56.	Visiting the graves	102
57.	Prayer said during a wind storm	103
58.	Supplication upon hearing thunder	104
59.	Supplication for rain	104
60.	Supplication said when it rains	105
61.	After rainfall	105
62.	Asking for clear skies	106
63.	Upon sighting the crescent moon	106
64.	Upon breaking fast	107
65.	Supplication before eating	107
66.	Upon completing the meal	108
67.	Supplication of the guest for the host	109
68.	Supplication said to one offering a drink or to one who intended to do that	110
69.	Supplication said when breaking fast in someone's home	110
70.	Supplication said by one fasting when presented with food and does not break	

	his fast	111
71.	Supplication said upon seeing the early or premature fruit	111
72.	Supplication said upon sneezing	111
73.	Supplication said to the newlywed	112
74.	The groom's supplication on the wedding night or when buying an animal	113
75.	Supplication before sexual intercourse	113
76.	When angry	114
77.	Supplication said upon seeing someone in trial or tribulation	114
78.	Remembrance said at a sitting or gathering…etc	115
79.	Supplication for the expiation of sins said at the conclusion of a sitting or gathering…etc	115
80.	Returning a supplication of forgiveness	116
81.	Supplication said to one who does you a favour	117
82.	Protection from the Dajjal	117
83.	Supplication said to one who pronounces his love for you, for Allah's sake	118
84.	Supplication said to one who has offered you some of his wealth	119
85.	Supplication said to the debtor when his	

	debt is settled	119
86.	Supplication for fear of shirk	119
87.	Returning a supplication after having bestowed a gift or charity upon someone	120
88.	Forbiddance of ascribing things to omens	121
89.	Supplication said when mounting an animal or any means of transport	121
90.	Supplication for travel	122
91.	Supplication upon entering a town or village…etc	124
92.	When entering the market	125
93.	Supplication for when the mounted animal (or mean of transport) stumbles	126
94.	Supplication of the traveller for the resident	126
95.	Supplication of the resident for the traveller	126
96.	Remembrance while ascending or descending	127
97.	Prayer of the traveller as dawn approaches	128
98.	Stopping or lodging somewhere	128
99.	While returning from travel	128
100.	What to say upon receiving pleasing or displeasing news	129
101.	Excellence of sending prayers upon the Prophet	130
102.	Excellence of spreading the Islamic greeting	131
103.	Supplication said upon hearing a rooster	

crow or the braying of an ass	132
104. Supplication upon hearing the barking of dogs at night	132
105. Supplication said for one you have insulted	132
106. The etiquette of praising a fellow Muslim	133
107. Supplication said between the Yemeni corner and the black stone (at the Kabah)	133
108. Supplication said when at Mount Safa & Mount Marwah	134
109. The Day of Arafah	135
110. At the Sacred Site (al-Mashar al-Haram)	136
111. When throwing each pebble at the Jamarat	136
112. At the black stone	137
113. Supplication made against an enemy	137
114. What to say when in fear of a people	137
115. What to say at times of amazement and delight	138
116. What to do upon receiving pleasant news	138
117. What to say and do when feeling some pain in the body	138
118. What to say when in fear of afflicting something or someone with one's eye	139
119. Etiquette of retiring for the night	140
120. The Talbiyah	140
121. What to say when startled	141

122. What is said to a disbeliever when he sneezes 141
123. Returning a greeting to a disbeliever 141
124. When insulted while fasting 142
125. When slaughtering or offering a sacrifice 142
126. What is said to ward off the deception of the obstinate Shaytans 142
127. Seeking forgiveness and repentance 143
128. Excellence of remembrance and glorification of Allah 145
129. How the prophet ﷺ made tasbih 152

1. When waking up

(1)

الْحَمْدُ لِلَّهِ الَّذِي أَحْيانا بَعْدَ ما أَماتَنا وَإِليهِ النُّشور

*Alhamdu lillahilladhi ahyana b'ada
ma amatana wa'ilayhin nushour*

'All praise is for Allah who gave us life after having taken it from us and unto Him is the resurrection'

(2)

The Prophet ﷺ said:

'Whoever awakes at night and then says:

لا إلهَ إلاّ اللَّهُ وَحْدَهُ لا شَريكَ له، لهُ المُلْكُ ولهُ الحَمد، وهوَ على كلِّ شيءٍ قدير، سُبْحانَ اللَّهِ، والحمدُ لله، ولا إلهَ إلاّ اللَّهُ واللَّهُ أكبَر، وَلا حَوْلَ وَلا قوّة إلاّ بِاللَّهِ العليّ العظيم

La ilaha illallahu wahdahu la sharika lah, lahulmulku walahulhamd, wahuwa 'ala kulli shay'in qadir, subhanallah, walhamdu lillah, wala ilaha illallah wallahu akbar, wala hawla wala quwwata illa billahil'aliyyil adheem

'None has the right to be worshipped except Allah, alone without associate, to Him belongs sovereignty and praise and He is over all things wholly capable How perfect Allah is, and all praise is for Allah, and none has the right to be worshipped except Allah, Allah is the greatest

and there is no power nor might except with Allah, The Most High, The Supreme
…and then supplicates:

رَبِّ اغْفِرْ لي

Rabbighfir li

'O my Lord forgive me'
…will be forgiven'
al-Walid said, "or he ﷺ said:
'and then asks, he will be answered if he then performs ablution and prays, his prayer will be accepted'"

(3)

الحمدُ لله الذي عافاني في جَسَدي وَرَدَّ عَلَيَّ روحي وَأَذِنَ لي بِذِكْرِه

*Alhamdu lillahilladhi 'afani fi jasadi
waradda 'alayya ruhi wa adhina li bidhikrih*

'All praise is for Allah who restored to me my health and returned my soul and has allowed me to remember Him'

(4)

﴿إنَّ في خَلْقِ السَّمَوَاتِ وَالأَرْضِ واخْتِـلافِ اللَّيـلِ والنهارِ لآياتٍ لأُولي الألباب﴾

(سورة ال عمران 190 - 200)

*Inna fi khalqis samawati wal ardi waikhtilafil layli
Wannaharil ayatin li ulil albaab…*

(From Verse 3:190 till the end of the chapter Ali Aimran)

2. Supplication when wearing a garment

(5)

الحمدُ لله الَذِي كَسانِي هذا (الثوبَ) وَرَزَقَنيهِ
مِنْ غَيْـرِ حَولٍ مِنّي وَلا قوّةٍ

Alhamdu lillahilladhi kasani hadha (aththawb) warazaqanihi min ghayri hawlin minni wala quwwah

'All Praise is for Allah who has clothed me with this garment and provided it for me, with no power nor might from myself'

3. Supplication said when wearing a new garment

(6)

اللّهُـمَّ لَـكَ الحَمْـدُ أنْـتَ كَسَـوْتَنيهِ، أَسْأَلُكَ مِـنْ خَيـرِهِ وَخَيْرِ مَا صُنِعَ لَـهُ، وَأَعوذُ بِكَ مِـنْ شَرِّهِ وَشَرِّ ما صُنِعَ لَهُ

Allahumma lakalhamdu anta kasawtanih, as'aluka min khayrihi wakhayri ma suni'a lah, wa a'udhu bika min sharrihi washarri ma sunia lah

'O Allah, for You is all praise, You have clothed me with it (i.e. the garment), I ask You for the good of it and the good for which it was made, and I seek refuge with You from the evil of it and the evil for which it was made'

4. Supplication said to someone wearing a new garment

(7)

تُبْلـي وَيُخْلِفُ اللَّهُ تَعَالى

Tubli wayukhlifullahu t'ala

'May you wear it out and Allah ﷻ replace it (with another).' The intended meaning: A supplication for long life"

(8)

اِلبَس جَديـداً وَعِـشْ حَميداً وَمُـتْ شهيداً

Ilbas jadidan w'aish hamidan wamut shahidan

'Wear anew, live commendably and die a *shaheed*'

Shaheed: One who dies fighting the disbelievers in order to make the word of Allah superior or in defense of Islam. It also has other meanings found in the Sunnah such as: the one who dies defending his life, wealth or family; the woman who passes away due to childbirth; one who drowns…etc

5. Before undressing

(9)

بِسْمِ اللَّه

Bismillah

'In the name of Allah'

6. Before entering the toilet

(10)

(بِسْمِ اللهِ) اللَّهُمَّ إِنِّي أَعوذُ بِكَ مِنَ الْخُبْثِ وَالْخَبَائِثِ

(Bismillah) allahumma inni a'udhu bika minalkhubthi wal khaba'ith

'(In the name of Allah) O Allah, I take refuge with you from all evil and evildoers'

7. After leaving the toilet

(11)

غُفْرانَك

Ghufranak

'I ask You (Allah) for forgiveness'

8. When starting ablution

(12)

بِسْمِ اللهِ

Bismillah

'In the name of Allah'

9. Upon completing the ablution

(13)

أَشْهَدُ أَنْ لا إِلَـهَ إِلاَّ اللهُ وَحْدَهُ لا شَرِيـكَ لَـهُ وَأَشْهَدُ أَنَّ مُحَمَّداً عَبْدُهُ وَرَسُولُه

Ashhadu an la ilaha illallahu wahdahu la sharika lah, waashhadu anna Muhammadan abduhu warasuluh

'I bear witness that none has the right to be worshipped except Allah, alone without partner, and I bear witness that Muhammad is His slave and Messenger'

(14)

اللَّهُمَّ اجْعَلني مِنَ التَّـوَّابِينَ وَاجْعَلْني مِنَ المتَطَهِّرين

Allahummaj'alni minattawwabena waj'alni minalmutatahhiren

'O Allah, make me of those who return to You often in repentance and make me of those who remain clean and pure

(15)

سُبْحَـانَكَ اللَّهُـمَّ وَبِحَمدك أَشْهَدُ أَنْ لا إِلهَ إِلاَّ أَنْتَ أَسْتَغْفِرُكَ وَأَتوبُ إِلَـيْك

Subhanak allahumma wabihamdika ashhadu an la ilaha illa anta astaghfiruka wa atobu ilayk

'How perfect You are O Allah, and I praise You, I bear witness that none has the right to be

worshipped except You, I seek Your forgiveness
and turn in repentance to You'

10. When leaving the home

(16)

بِسْمِ اللهِ، تَوَكَّلْتُ عَلَى اللهِ وَلَا حَوْلَ وَلَا قُوَّةَ إِلَّا بِاللهِ

*Bismillah, tawakkaltu 'alallah, wala hawla
wala quwwata illa billah*

'In the name of Allah, I place my trust in
Allah, and there is no might nor power
except with Allah'

(17)

اللَّهُمَّ إِنِّي أَعُوذُ بِكَ أَنْ أَضِلَّ أَوْ أُضَلَّ، أَوْ أَزِلَّ أَوْ أُزَلَّ، أَوْ
أَظْلِمَ أَوْ أُظْلَمَ، أَوْ أَجْهَلَ أَوْ يُجْهَلَ عَلَيّ

*Allahumma inni a'udhu bika an adilla aw udall,
aw azilla aw ozall, aw adhlima aw udhlam,
aw ajhala aw yujhala 'alay.*

'O Allah, I take refuge with You lest I should stray
or be led astray, or slip or be tripped, or oppress
or be oppressed, or behave foolishly or be treated
foolishly' slip: i.e. to commit a sin unintentionally

11. Upon entering the home

(18)

بِسْمِ اللهِ وَلَجْنَا، وَبِسْمِ اللهِ خَرَجْنَا، وَعَلَى رَبِّنَا تَوَكَّلْنَا

Bismillahi walajna, wabismillahi kharajna, w'ala rabbina tawakkalna

'In the name of Allah we enter and in the name of Allah we leave, and upon our Lord we place our trust'

12. Supplication when going to the mosque

(19)

اللَّهُمَّ اجْعَلْ فِي قَلْبِي نُورًا، وَفِي لِسَانِي نُورًا، وَاجْعَلْ فِي سَمْعِي نُورًا، وَاجْعَلْ فِي بَصَرِي نُورًا، وَاجْعَلْ مِنْ خَلْفِي نُورًا، وَمِنْ أَمَامِي نُورًا، وَاجْعَلْ مِنْ فَوْقِي نُورًا، وَمِنْ تَحْتِي نُورًا. اللَّهُمَّ أَعْطِنِي نُورًا

Allahumma ij'al fi qalbi nura, wafi lisani nura, waj'al fi sam'i nura, waj'al fi basare nura, waj'al min khalfi nura, wamin amami nura, waj'al min fawqi nura, wamin tahte nura, allahumma atini nura

'O Allah, place within my heart light, and upon my tongue light, and within my ears light, and within my eyes light, and place behind me light and in front of me light and above me light and beneath me light. O Allah, bestow upon me light'

13. Upon entering the mosque

(20)

أَعُوذُ بِاللهِ الْعَظِيمِ وَبِوَجْهِهِ الْكَرِيمِ وَسُلْطَانِهِ الْقَدِيمِ مِنَ الشَّيْطَانِ الرَّجِيمِ، [بِسْمِ اللهِ، وَالصَّلَاةُ] [وَالسَّلَامُ عَلَى رَسُولِ اللهِ]، اللَّهُمَّ افْتَحْ لِي أَبْوَابَ رَحْمَتِكَ

A'udhu billahil adheem wabiwajhihil kareem wasultanihil qadeem minashshaytanir rajeem, [bismillah, wassalatu] [wassalamu 'ala rasulillah], allahumma iftah li abwaba rahmatik

'I take refuge with Allah, The Supreme and with His Noble Face, and His eternal authority from the accursed devil. In the name of Allah, and prayers and peace be upon the Messenger of Allah O Allah, open the gates of Your mercy for me'

14. Upon leaving the mosque

(21)

بِسْمِ اللهِ وَالصَّلَاةُ وَالسَّلَامُ عَلَى رَسُولِ اللهِ، اللَّهُمَّ إِنِّي أَسْأَلُكَ مِنْ فَضْلِكَ، اللَّهُمَّ اعْصِمْنِي مِنَ الشَّيْطَانِ الرَّجِيمِ

Bismillah wassalatu wassalamu 'ala rasulillah, allahumma inni as'aluka min fadlik, allahumma i'simny minashshaytanir rajeem

'In the name of Allah, and prayers and peace be upon the Messenger of Allah. O Allah, I ask You from Your favour O Allah, guard me from the accursed devil'

15. Supplications related to the adhan (the call to prayer)

(22)

'One repeats just as the muadhdhin (one who calls to prayer) says, except when he says:

حَيَّ عَلَى الصَّلاةِ (أَوْ) حَيَّ عَلَى الْفَلاحِ

Hayya 'alas salah (or) hayya 'alal falah

'come to prayer, come to success'
instead, one should say:

لا حَوْلَ وَلا قُوَّةَ إِلاَّ بِاللهِ

La hawla wala quwwata illa billah

'There is no might nor power except with Allah'

(23)

Immediately following the declaration of faith called by the muadhdhin, one says:

وَأَنَا أَشْهَدُ أَنْ لا إِلَهَ إِلاَّ اللهُ وَحْدَهُ لا شَرِيكَ لَهُ، وَأَنَّ مُحَمَّداً عَبْدُهُ وَرَسُولُهُ، رَضِيتُ بِاللهِ رَبًّا، وَبِمُحَمَّدٍ رَسُولاً وَبِالإِسْلامِ دِيناً

Waana ashhadu an la ilaha illallahu wahdahu la sharika lah, wa anna Muhammadan abduhu warasuluh, radetu billahi rabban wabimuhammadin rasulan wabil islami dena

'And I too bear witness that none has the

right to be worshipped except Allah, alone,
without partner, and that Muhammad is His
salve and Messenger I am pleased with Allah
as a Lord, and Muhammad as a Messenger
and Islam as a religion'

(24)

'One should then send prayers on the Prophet ﷺ
after answering the call of the *muadhdhin*'

(25)

اللهُـمَّ رَبَّ هَذِهِ الدَّعْـوَةِ التَّامَّة وَالصَّلاةِ القَائِمَة آتِ
مُحَـمَّداً الوَسِيـلَةَ وَالفَضِيـلَة وَابْعَـثْـهُ مَقَامـاً مَحمـوداً الَّذي
وَعَـدتَه إنَّكَ لا تُخلِفُ الميعاد

*Allahumma rabba hadhihid d'awatit tammah, wassalatil
qa'imah ati Muhammadan alwasilata walfadilah,
wab'athhu maqaman mahmudan alladhi w'adtah,
innaka la tukhliful me'ad*

'O Allah, Owner of this perfect call and Owner
of this prayer to be performed, bestow upon
Muhammad *alwasilah* and *alfadilah* and send him
upon a praised platform which You have promised
him Verily, You never fail in Your promise'

alwasilah: A station in paradise
alfadilah: A rank above the rest of creation
praised platform: One in which all of creation

will praise him on, in order to bring about the account quickly and be relieved from the lengthy standing *or* the role of intercession

(26)

One should also supplicate for himself during the time between the adhan and the iqamah as supplication at such time is not rejected

16. Supplication at the start of the prayer (after takbir)

(27)

اللّهُـمَّ باعِـدْ بَيْـني وَبَيْنَ خَطايايَ كَما باعَدْتَ بَيْنَ المَشْرِقِ وَالمَغْرِب، اللّهُـمَّ نَقِّـني مِنْ خَطايايَ كَما يُـنَقَّى الثَّوْبُ الأَبْيَضُ مِنَ الدَّنَس، اللّهُـمَّ اغْسِلْني مِنْ خَطايايَ بِالثَّلْجِ وَالماءِ وَالبَرَدْ

Allahumma b'aid bayni wabayna khatayaya kama b'adta baynal mashriqi walmaghrib, allahumma naqqini min khatayaya kama yunaqqath thawbul abyadu minaddanas, allahummagh silni min khatayaya bith thalji walma'ai walbarad

'O Allah, distance me from my sins just as You have distanced the East from the West, O Allah, purify me of my sins as a white robe is purified of filth, O Allah, cleanse me of my sins with snow, water, and ice'

(28)

سُبْحَانَكَ اللَّهُمَّ وَبِحَمْدِكَ وَتَبَارَكَ اسْمُكَ وَتَعَالَى جَدُّكَ وَلَا إِلَهَ غَيْرُكَ

Subhanakallahumma wabihamdika watabarakasmuka wat'ala jadduka wala ilaha ghayruk

'How perfect You are O Allah, and I praise You. Blessed be Your name, and lofty is Your position and none has the right to be worshipped except You'

(29)

وَجَّهْتُ وَجْهِيَ لِلَّذِي فَطَرَ السَّمَوَاتِ وَالْأَرْضَ حَنِيفاً وَمَا أَنَا مِنَ الْمُشْرِكِينَ، إِنَّ صَلَاتِي، وَنُسُكِي، وَمَحْيَايَ، وَمَمَاتِي للهِ رَبِّ الْعَالَمِينَ، لَا شَرِيكَ لَهُ وَبِذَلِكَ أُمِرْتُ وَأَنَا مِنَ الْمُسْلِمِينَ. اللَّهُمَّ أَنْتَ الْمَلِكُ لَا إِلَهَ إِلَّا أَنْتَ، أَنْتَ رَبِّي وَأَنَا عَبْدُكَ، ظَلَمْتُ نَفْسِي وَاعْتَرَفْتُ بِذَنْبِي فَاغْفِرْ لِي ذُنُوبِي جَمِيعاً إِنَّهُ لَا يَغْفِرُ الذُّنُوبَ إِلَّا أَنْتَ. وَاهْدِنِي لِأَحْسَنِ الْأَخْلَاقِ لَا يَهْدِي لِأَحْسَنِهَا إِلَّا أَنْتَ، وَاصْرِفْ عَنِّي سَيِّئَهَا، لَا يَصْرِفُ عَنِّي سَيِّئَهَا إِلَّا أَنْتَ، لَبَّيْكَ وَسَعْدَيْكَ، وَالْخَيْرُ كُلُّهُ بِيَدَيْكَ، وَالشَّرُّ لَيْسَ إِلَيْكَ، أَنَا بِكَ وَإِلَيْكَ، تَبَارَكْتَ وَتَعَالَيْتَ أَسْتَغْفِرُكَ وَأَتُوبُ إِلَيْكَ

Wajjahtu wajhiya lilladhi fataras samawati walarda hanifan wama ana minal mushrikeen, inna salati wanusuki wamahyaya wamamati lillahi rabbilalameen, la sharika lahu wabidhalika umirtu wa ana minal muslimeen. Allahumma antal maliku la ilaha illa ant, anta rabbi wa ana abduk, dhalamtu nafsi w'ataraftu bidhanbe faghfir li dhunubu jame'an innahu la yaghfirudh dhunubu illa ant. Wahdini liahsanil akhlaqi la yahdi li ahsaniha illa ant, wasrif anni sayyi'aha la yasrifu anni sayyi'aha illa ant, labbayka wa'adayk, walkhayru kulluhu biyadayk, washsharru laysa ilayk, ana bika wa'ilayk, tabarakta wat'alayt, astaghfiruka wa atubu ilayk

'I have turned my face sincerely towards He who has brought forth the heavens and the Earth and I am not of those who associate (others with Allah). Indeed my prayer, my sacrifice, my life and my death are for Allah, Lord of the worlds, no partner has He, with this I am commanded and I am of the Muslims O Allah, You are the Sovereign, none has the right to be worshipped except You. You are my Lord and I am Your servant, I have wronged my own soul and have acknowledged my sin, so forgive me all my sins for no one forgives sins except You. Guide me to the best of characters for none can guide to it other than You, and deliver me from the worst of characters for none can deliver me from it other than You. Here I am, in answer to Your call, happy to serve you. All good is within Your hands and evil does not stem from You. I exist by your will and will return to you. Blessed and High are You, I seek Your forgiveness and repent unto You'

Allah does not create pure evil which does not

have any good or contain any benefit, wisdom or mercy at all, nor does He punish anyone without having commited a sin. Something can be good in terms of its creation when viewed in a particular perspective and at the same time be evil when viewed in another way. Allah created the devil and by him, He tests His servants, so there are those who hate the devil, fight him and his way and they stand at enmity towards him and his followers and there are others who are at allegiance with the devil and follow his steps. So evil exists in His creatures by His will and wisdom, not in His actions or act of creating.

(30)

اللَّهُمَّ رَبَّ جِبْرَائِيل، وَمِيكَائِيل، وَإِسْرَافِيل، فَاطِرَ السَّمواتِ وَالأَرْضِ، عَالِمَ الغَيْبِ وَالشَّهَادَةِ أَنْتَ تَحْكُمُ بَيْنَ عِبَادِكَ فِيمَا كَانُوا فِيهِ يَخْتَلِفُون. اهْدِنِي لِمَا اخْتُلِفَ فِيهِ مِنَ الْحَقِّ بِإِذْنِكَ، إِنَّكَ تَهْدِي مَنْ تَشَاءُ إِلَى صِرَاطٍ مُسْتَقِيم

Allahumma rabba jibrael, wa mik'ail, wa israfel fatiras samawati wal ard, alimal ghaybi washshahadah, anta tah kumu bayna 'ibadika fima kanu fihi yakhtalifun ihdini limakhtulifa fihi minal haqqi bi'idhnik, innaka tahdi man tash'au ila siratin mustaqeem

'O Allah, Lord of *Jibrael*, *Mikaeel* and *Israfeel* (great angles), Creator of the heavens and the Earth, Knower of the seen and the unseen.

You are the arbitrator between Your servants in that which they have disputed Guide me to the truth by Your leave, in that which they have differed, for verily You guide whom You will to a straight path'

(31)

اللهُ أَكْبَرُ كَبِيرا، اللهُ أَكْبَرُ كَبِيرا، اللهُ أَكْبَرُ كَبِيرا، وَالْحَمْدُ لِلهِ كَثِيرا، وَالْحَمْدُ لِلهِ كَثِيرا، وَالْحَمْدُ لِلهِ كَثِيرا، وَسُبْحَانَ اللهِ بُكْرَةً وَأَصِيلا. (ثلاثا)

أَعُوذُ بِاللهِ مِنَ الشَّيْطَانِ مِنْ نَفْخِهِ وَنَفْثِهِ وَهَمْزِه

Allahu akbaru kabera, allahu akbaru kabera, allahu akbaru kabera, walhamdu lillahi kathera, walhamdu lillahi kathera, walhamdu lillahi kathera, wa subhanallahi bukratan wa asela

(three times)

a'udhu billahi minash shaytani min nafkhihi wa nafthihi wa hamzih

'Allah is Most Great, Allah is Most Great, Allah is Most Great, much praise is for Allah, much praise is for Allah, much praise is for Allah, and I declare the perfection of Allah in the early morning and in the late afternoon' (three times)
'I take refuge with Allah from the devil, from his pride, his poetry and his madness'

(32)

The prophet ﷺ would say (as an opening supplication in prayer) when rising from sleep to perform prayers during the night:

اللّٰهُمَّ لَكَ الْحَمْدُ أَنْتَ نُورُ السَّمٰوَاتِ وَالْأَرْضِ وَمَنْ فِيهِنَّ، وَلَكَ الْحَمْدُ أَنْتَ قَيِّمُ السَّمٰوَاتِ وَالْأَرْضِ وَمَنْ فِيهِنَّ، [وَلَكَ الْحَمْدُ أَنْتَ رَبُّ السَّمٰوَاتِ وَالْأَرْضِ وَمَنْ فِيهِنَّ] [وَلَكَ الْحَمْدُ لَكَ مُلْكُ السَّمٰوَاتِ وَالْأَرْضِ وَمَنْ فِيهِنَّ] [وَلَكَ الْحَمْدُ أَنْتَ مَلِكُ السَّمٰوَاتِ وَالْأَرْضِ] [وَلَكَ الْحَمْدُ] [أَنْتَ الْحَقُّ وَوَعْدُكَ الْحَقُّ، وَقَوْلُكَ الْحَقُّ، وَلِقَاؤُكَ الْحَقُّ، وَالْجَنَّةُ حَقٌّ، وَالنَّارُ حَقٌّ، وَالنَّبِيُّونَ حَقٌّ، وَمُحَمَّدٌ حَقٌّ، وَالسَّاعَةُ حَقٌّ] [اللّٰهُمَّ لَكَ أَسْلَمْتُ، وَعَلَيْكَ تَوَكَّلْتُ، وَبِكَ آمَنْتُ، وَإِلَيْكَ أَنَبْتُ، وَبِكَ خَاصَمْتُ، وَإِلَيْكَ حَاكَمْتُ. فَاغْفِرْ لِي مَا قَدَّمْتُ، وَمَا أَخَّرْتُ، وَمَا أَسْرَرْتُ، وَمَا أَعْلَنْتُ] [أَنْتَ الْمُقَدِّمُ وَأَنْتَ الْمُؤَخِّرُ، لَا إِلٰهَ إِلَّا أَنْتَ] [أَنْتَ إِلٰهِي لَا إِلٰهَ إِلَّا أَنْتَ]

Allahumma lakalhamd anta norussamawati wal ardi waman fihin, walakalhamd, anta qayyimussamawati wal ardi waman fihin, [walakalhamd, anta rabbussamawati wal ardi waman fihin], [walakalhamd, laka mulkussamawati wal ardi waman fihin] [walakalhamd, anta malikussamawati wal ard] [walakalhamd] [antalhaq, wawadukalhaq, waqawlukalhaq, waliqaokalhaq, waljannatu haq wannaru haq, wannabiyyona haq, wa Muhammadun ﷺ haq, wass'atu haq] [allahumma laka aslamt, wa 'alayka tawakkalt, wabika amant, wa ilayka anabt, wabika khasamt, wa ilayka hakamt, faghfir li ma

*qaddamt, wama akhkhart, wama asrart, wama 'alant]
[antalmuqaddim, wa antalmuakhkhir, la ilaha illa
ant] [anta ilahi la ilaha illa ant*

'O Allah, to You belongs all praise, You are the
Light of the heavens and the Earth and all that
is within them To You belongs all praise, You are
the Sustainer of the heavens and the Earth and
all that is within them To You belongs all praise
You are Lord of the heavens and the Earth and all
that is within them To You belongs all praise and
the kingdom of the heavens and the Earth and
all that is within them To You belongs all praise,
You are the King of the heavens and the Earth
and to You belongs all praise You are The Truth,
Your promise is true, your Word is true, and the
Day in which we will encounter You is true, the
Garden of Paradise is true and the Fire is true,
and the Prophets are true, Muhammad ﷺ is true
and the Final Hour is true O Allah, unto You I
have submitted, and upon You I have relied, and
in You I have believed, and to You I have turned
in repentance, and over You I have disputed, and
to You I have turned for judgment So forgive me
for what has come to pass of my sins and what
will come to pass, and what I have hidden and
what I have made public You are *al-Muqaddim*
and *al-Muakhkhir* None has the right to be

worshipped except You, You are my Deity, none has the right to be worshipped except You'

Meaning of *al-Muqaddim* and *al-Muakhkhir*: Allah puts forward and favours whom He wills from amongst His creation just as He defers and holds back whom He wills in accordance to His wisdom Eg Favouring man over the rest of creation, favouring the Prophets over the rest of mankind, favouring Muhammad ﷺ over all the Prophets and Messengers…etc

17. While bowing in prayer (*ruku'*)

(33)

سُبْحانَ رَبِّيَ العَظيم (ثلاثًا)

Subhana rabbiyal adheem (three times)

'How perfect my Lord is, The Supreme' (three times)

(34)

سُبْحانَكَ اللّهُمَّ رَبَّنا وَبِحَمْدِك، اللّهُمَّ اغْفِرْ لي

Subhanakal lahumma rabbana wabihamdik, allahummaghfir li

'How perfect You are O Allah, our Lord and I praise You O Allah, forgive me'

(35)

سُبُّوحٌ قُدُّوسٌ، رَبُّ الملائِكَةِ وَالرُّوح

Subbuhun quddus, rabbul mala'ikati warruh

'Perfect and Holy (He is), Lord of the angles and the *Ruh* (i.e. Jibrael)'

(36)

اللَّهُمَّ لَكَ رَكَعْتُ وَبِكَ آمَنْتُ، وَلَكَ أَسْلَمْتُ، خَشَعَ لَكَ سَمْعِي، وَبَصَرِي، وَمُخِّي، وَعَظْمِي، وَعَصَبِي، وَمَا اسْتَقَلَّ بِهِ قَدَمِي

Allahumma laka raka't, wabika amant, walaka aslamt, khasha laka sami'i, wabasari, wamukhkhi, wa'adhmi, wa'asabi, wamastaqallah bihi qadami

'O Allah, unto You I have bowed, and in You I have believed, and to You I have submitted My hearing, sight, mind, bones, tendons and what my feet carry are humbled before You'

(37)

سُبْحانَ ذِي الْجَبَرُوت، والمَلَكُوت، وَالكِبْرِياء، وَالْعَظَمَه

Subhana dhil jabarut, walmalakut, wal kibriya, wal'adhamah

'How perfect He is, The Possessor of total power, sovereignty, magnificence and grandeur'

18. Upon rising from the bowing position

(38)

سَمِعَ اللَّهُ لِمَنْ حَمِدَهُ

Sami'allahu liman hamidah

'May Allah answer he who praises Him'

This supplication is to be made *while* rising

(39)

رَبَّنَا وَلَكَ الحَمْدُ حَمْداً كَثِيراً طَيِّباً مُبَارَكاً فِيهِ

Rabbana walakalhamdu hamdan kathiran tayyiban mubarakan fih

'Our Lord, for You is all praise, an abundant beautiful blessed praise'

(40)

مِلْءَ السَّمواتِ وَمِلْءَ الأَرْض، وَما بَيْنَهُما، وَمِلْءَ ما شِئْتَ مِنْ شَيْءٍ بَعْدُ. أَهْلَ الثَّناءِ وَالمَجْدِ، أَحَقُّ ما قالَ العَبْدُ، وَكُلُّنا لَكَ عَبْدٌ. اللَّهُمَّ لا مانِعَ لِما أَعْطَيْت، وَلا مُعْطِيَ لِما مَنَعْت، وَلا يَنْفَعُ ذا الجَدِّ مِنْكَ الجَدُّ

Mil'as samawati wamil'al ard, wama baynahuma, wamil'a ma shi'ta min shay'in b'ad, ahlath thana'i walmajd, ahaqqu ma qalal 'abd, wakulluna laka 'abd Allahumma la mania' lima atayt, wala mu'tiya lima man'at, wala yanf'au dhaljaddi minkaljad

'The heavens and the Earth and all between them abound with Your praises, and all that You will

abounds with Your praises O Possessor of praise and majesty, the truest thing a slave has said (of You) and we are all Your slaves O Allah, none can prevent what You have willed to bestow and none can bestow what You have willed to prevent, and no wealth or majesty can benefit anyone, as from You is all wealth and majesty'
This supplication is made optionally only in conjunction with the previous one

19. Supplication whilst prostrating (sujood)

(41)

سُبْحَانَ رَبِّيَ الأَعْلَى (ثلاثا)

Subhana rabbiyal 'ala (three times)

'How perfect my Lord is,
The Most High' (three times)

(42)

سُبْحَانَكَ اللَّهُمَّ رَبَّنَا وَبِحَمْدِكَ، اللَّهُمَّ اغْفِرْ لِي

Subhanakal lahumma rabbana wabihamdik, allahummagh fir li

'How perfect You are O Allah, our Lord, and I praise You O Allah, forgive me'

(43)

سُبُّوحٌ قُدُّوسٌ، رَبُّ المَلائِكَةِ وَالرُّوح

Subbuhun quddus, rabbul mala'ikati warruh
'Perfect and Holy (He is), Lord of the angles and the *Ruh* (i.e. Jibrael)'

(44)

اللهُمَّ لَكَ سَجَدْتُ وَبِكَ آمَنْتُ، وَلَكَ أَسْلَمْتُ، سَجَدَ وَجْهِي لِلَّذِي خَلَقَهُ وَصَوَّرَهُ وَشَقَّ سَمْعَهُ وَبَصَرَهُ، تَبَارَكَ اللهُ أَحْسَنُ الخَالِقِين

Allahumma laka sajadt, wabika amant, walaka aslamt, sajada wajhi lilladhi khalaqahu wasawwarahu washaqqa samahu wabasarahu, tabarakallahu ahsanul khaliqin

'O Allah, unto You I have prostrated and in You I have believed, and unto You I have submitted My face has prostrated before He Who created it and fashioned it, and brought forth its faculties of hearing and seeing Blessed is Allah, the Best of creators'

(45)

سُبْحَانَ ذِي الْجَبَرُوتِ، وَالْمَلَكُوتِ، وَالْكِبْرِيَاءِ، وَالْعَظَمَه

Subhana dhiljabarut, walmalakut, walkibriya, wal'adhamah

'How perfect He is, The Possessor of total power, sovereignty, magnificence and grandeur'

(46)

اللَّهُمَّ اغْفِرْ لِي ذَنْبِي كُلَّهُ، دِقَّهُ وَجِلَّهُ، وَأَوَّلَهُ وَآخِرَه

وَعَلَانِيَّتَهُ وَسِرَّهُ

Allahummaghfir li dhanbi kullah, diqqahu wajillah, waawwalahu waakhirah, wa 'alaniyyatahu wasirrah

'O Allah, forgive me all of my sins, the small and great of them, the first and last of them, and the seen and hidden of them'

(47)

اللَّهُمَّ إِنِّي أَعـوذُ بِرِضـاكَ مِنْ سَخَطِكَ، وَبِمعـافـاتِكَ مِنْ عُقوبَـتِك، وَأَعـوذُ بِكَ مِنْك، لا أُحْصـي ثَنـاءً عَلَيْك، أَنْـتَ كَما أَثْنَيْتَ عَلى نَفْسِك

Allahumma inni a'udhu biridaka min sakhatik, wabimu'afatika min uqubatiq, wa a'udhu bika mink, la uhsi thanaan 'alayk, anta kama athnayta 'ala nafsik

'O Allah, I take refuge within Your pleasure from Your displeasure and within Your pardon from Your punishment, and I take refuge in You from You I cannot enumerate Your praise, You are as You have praised Yourself'

20. Supplication between the two prostrations

(48)

رَبِّ اغْفِـرْ لي، رَبِّ اغْفِـرْ لي

Rabbighfir li, rabbighfir li

'My Lord forgive me, My Lord forgive me'

(49)

اللَّهُمَّ اغْفِرْ لِي، وَارْحَمْنِي، وَاهْدِنِي، وَاجْبُرْنِي،
وَعَافِنِي وَارْزُقْنِي وَارْفَعْنِي

*Allahummaghfir li, warhamni, wahdini, wajburni,
w'afini, warzuqni warf'ani*

'O Allah, forgive me, have mercy upon me,
guide me, enrich me, give me health, grant me
sustenance and raise my rank'

21. Supplication when prostrating due to recitation of the Quran

(50)

سَجَدَ وَجْهِيَ لِلَّذِي خَلَقَهُ، وَشَقَّ سَمْعَهُ وَبَصَرَهُ، بِحَوْلِهِ وَقُوَّتِهِ،
فَتَبَارَكَ اللهُ أَحْسَنُ الْخَالِقِي

*Sajada wajhe lilladhi khalaqahu washaqqa samahu
wabasarahu bihawlihi waquwwatih
{tabaraka Allahu ahsanu alkhaliqin}*

'My face fell prostrate before He who created
it and brought forth its faculties of hearing and
seeing by His might and power So Blessed is
Allah, the best of creators

(51)

اللَّهُمَّ اكْتُبْ لِي بِهَا عِنْدَكَ أَجْرًا، وَضَعْ عَنِّي بِهَا وِزْرًا، وَاجْعَلْهَا لِي
عِنْدَكَ ذُخْرًا، وَتَقَبَّلْهَا مِنِّي كَمَا تَقَبَّلْتَهَا مِنْ عَبْدِكَ داود

Allahumm aktub li biha aindaka ajra, wad'a anni biha

wizra, waj'alha li indaka dhukhra, wataqabbalha minni kama taqabbaltaha min abdika Dawud

'O Allah, record for me a reward for this (prostration), and remove from me a sin Save it for me and accept it from me just as You had accepted it from Your servant Dawud'

22. The Tashahhud

Tashahhud: what one says in the sitting position in prayer

(52)

التَّحِيَّاتُ لِلهِ وَالصَّلَوَاتُ وَالطَّيِّبَاتُ، السَّلَامُ عَلَيْكَ أَيُّهَا النَّبِيُّ وَرَحْمَةُ اللهِ وَبَرَكَاتُهُ، السَّلَامُ عَلَيْنَا وَعَلَى عِبَادِكَ الصَّالِحِينَ. أَشْهَدُ أَنْ لَا إِلَهَ إِلَّا اللهُ، وَأَشْهَدُ أَنَّ مُحَمَّداً عَبْدُهُ وَرَسُولُهُ

Attahiyyatu lillahi wassalawatu wattayyibat, assalamu 'alayka ayyuhan nabiyyu warahmatullahi wabarakatuh, assalamu 'alayna wala 'ibadillahis salihin ashhadu an la ilaha illallah, wa ashhadu anna Muhammadan abduhu warasuluh

'Attahiyyat is for Allah All acts of worship and good deeds are for Him Peace and the mercy and blessings of Allah be upon you O Prophet Peace be upon us and all of Allah's righteous servants

I bear witness that none has the right to be worshipped except Allah and I bear witness that

Muhammad is His slave and Messenger'

Attahiyyat: all words which indicate the glorification of Allah, His eternal existence, His perfection and His sovereignty.

23. Prayers upon the Prophet ﷺ after the tashahhud

(53)

اللَّهُمَّ صَلِّ عَلَى مُحَمَّدٍ، وَعَلَى آلِ مُحَمَّدٍ، كَمَا صَلَّيْتَ عَلَى إِبْرَاهِيمَ وَعَلَى آلِ إِبْرَاهِيمَ، إِنَّكَ حَمِيدٌ مَجِيد، اللَّهُمَّ بَارِكْ عَلَى مُحَمَّدٍ، وَعَلَى آلِ مُحَمَّدٍ، كَمَا بَارَكْتَ عَلَى إِبْرَاهِيمَ وَعَلَى آلِ إِبْرَاهِيمَ، إِنَّكَ حَمِيدٌ مَجِيد

Allahumma salli 'ala Muhammad, w'aala ali Muhammad, kama sallayta 'ala Ibrahema w'aala ali Ibrahem, innaka hamedun majeed, allahumma barik 'ala Muhammad, w'aala ali Muhammad, kama barakta 'ala Ibrahema w'aala ali Ibrahem, innaka hamedun majeed

'O Allah, send prayers upon Muhammad and the followers of Muhammad, just as You sent prayers upon Ibrahem and upon the followers of Ibrahem Verily, You are full of praise and majesty O Allah, send blessings upon Mohammad and upon the family of Muhammad, just as You sent blessings upon Ibrahem and upon the family of Ibrahem Verily, You are full of praise and majesty'

send prayers: praise and exalt him in the highest and superior of gatherings: that of the closest angels to Allah

(al) has been translated in it's broadest sense: some scholars are of the view that the meaning here is more specific and that it means: *his ﷺ followers from among his family*

(54)

اللَّهُمَّ صَلِّ عَلَى مُحَمَّدٍ وَعَلَى أَزْوَاجِهِ وَذُرِّيَّتِهِ، كَمَا صَلَّيْتَ عَلَى آلِ إِبْرَاهِيمَ. وَبَارِكْ عَلَى مُحَمَّدٍ وَعَلَى أَزْوَاجِهِ وَذُرِّيَّتِهِ، كَمَا بَارَكْتَ عَلَى آلِ إِبْرَاهِيمَ. إِنَّكَ حَمِيدٌ مَجِيد

Allahumma salli 'ala Muhammad w'ala azwajihi wadhurriyyatihi kama sallayta 'ala ali Ibrahem, wabarik 'ala Muhammad, w'ala azwajihi wadhurriyyatih, kama barakta 'ala ali Ibrahem innaka hamedun majeed

'O Allah, send prayers upon Muhammad and upon the wives and descendants of Muhammad, just as You sent prayers upon the family of Ibrahem, and send blessings upon Muhammad and upon the wives and descendants of Muhammad, just as You sent blessings upon the family of Ibrahem Verily, You are full of praise and majesty'

24. Supplication said after the last *tashahhud* and before *salam*

(55)

اللَّهُمَّ إِنِّي أَعـوذُ بِكَ مِـنْ عَذابِ القَـبْرِ، وَمِنْ عَذابِ جَهَنَّمَ، وَمِـنْ فِتْنَةِ المَحْيا وَالمَمَاتِ، وَمِـنْ شَرِّ فِتْنَةِ المَسيحِ الدَّجَّالِ

Allahumma inni a'udhu bika min adhabil qabr, wamin adhabi jahannam, wamin fitnatil mahya wal mamat, wamin shari fitnatil masehiddajjal

'O Allah, I take refuge in You from the punishment of the grave, from the torment of the Fire, from the trials and tribulations of life and death and from the evil affliction of Al Masih Ad Dajjal'

Al Masih Ad Dajjal: among the great signs of the last hour and the greatest trials to befall mankind, which every Prophet has warned about Most of mankind will follow him He will appear from Asbahan, Iran at the time when the Muslims will conquer Constantinople He will be given special powers and will make the truth seem false and vice versa He will claim to be righteous and then he will claim prophethood and finally, divinity From his features is that he will be blind in his right eye which is a definite proof that contradicts his claim to be Allah as it is a sign of imperfection The word *Kafir* will be written between his eyes which every believer, literate or illiterate will recognise

(56)

اللّهُمَّ إِنِّي أَعوذُ بِكَ مِنْ عَذابِ القَبْرِ، وَأَعوذُ بِكَ مِنْ فِتْنَةِ المَسيحِ الدَّجّالِ، وَأَعوذُ بِكَ مِنْ فِتْنَةِ المَحْيا وَالمَماتِ. اللّهُمَّ إِنِّي أَعوذُ بِكَ مِنَ المَأْثَمِ وَالمَغْرَمِ

Allahumma inni a'udhu bika min adhabilqabr, wa a'udhu bika min fitnatil masehiddajjal, wa a'udhu bika min fitnatil mahya wal mamat. Allahumma inni a'udhu bika minal m'athami wal maghram

'O Allah, I take refuge in You from the punishment of the grave, and I take refuge in You from the temptation and trial of Al Masih Ad Dajjal, and I take refuge in You from the trials and tribulations of life and death O Allah, I take refuge in You from sin and debt'

(57)

اللّهُمَّ إِنِّي ظَلَمْتُ نَفْسي ظُلْماً كَثيراً وَلا يَغْفِرُ الذُّنوبَ إِلاّ أَنْتَ، فَاغْفِرْ لي مَغْفِرَةً مِنْ عِنْدِكَ وَارْحَمْني، إِنَّكَ أَنْتَ الغَفورُ الرَّحيمُ

Allahumma inni dhalamtu nafsi dhulman kathiran wala yaghfiruth dhunuba illa ant, faghfir li maghfiratan min indik warhamni, innaka antal ghafurur rahim

'O Allah, I have indeed oppressed my soul excessively and none can forgive sin except

You, so forgive me a forgiveness from Yourself and have mercy upon me Surely, You are The MostForgiving, The MostMerciful'

From Yourself: i.e. from Your innermost grace without deserving it and a forgiveness which is befitting to your tremendous generosity

(58)

اللَّهُمَّ اغْفِرْ لِي مَا قَدَّمْتُ وَمَا أَخَّرْتُ، وَمَا أَسْرَرْتُ وَمَا أَعْلَنْتُ، وَمَا أَسْرَفْتُ، وَمَا أَنْتَ أَعْلَمُ بِهِ مِنِّي. أَنْتَ المُقَدِّمُ، وَأَنْتَ المُؤَخِّرُ لا إِلَهَ إِلَّا أَنْتَ

Allahum maghfir li ma qaddamtu, wama akhkhart, wama asrartu wama 'alant, wama asraftt, wama anta 'alamu bihi minni, antal muqaddimu wa antal muakhkhiru la ilaha illa ant

'O Allah, forgive me for those sins which have come to pass as well as those which shall come to pass, and those I have committed in secret as well as those I have made public, and where I have exceeded all bounds as well as those things about which You are more knowledgeable You are *al-Muqaddim* and *al-Muakhkhir* None has the right to be worshipped except You'

Meaning of *al-Muqaddim* and *al-Muakhkhir*: Allah puts forward and favours whom He wills from amongst His creation just as He defers and holds back whom He wills in accordance to His wisdom Eg Favouring man over the rest of creation, favouring the Prophets over the rest of mankind, favouring Muhammad ﷺ over all the Prophets and Messengers…etc

(59)

اللَّهُمَّ أَعِنِّي عَلَى ذِكْرِكَ وَشُكْرِكَ، وَحُسْنِ عِبَادَتِكَ

Allahumma a'inni 'ala dhikrik, washukrik, wahusni 'ibadatik

'O Allah, help me to remember You, to thank You, and to worship You in the best of manners'

(60)

اللَّهُمَّ إِنِّي أَعُوذُ بِكَ مِنَ البُخْلِ، وَأَعُوذُ بِكَ مِنَ الجُبْنِ، وَأَعُوذُ بِكَ مِنْ أَنْ أُرَدَّ إِلَى أَرْذَلِ العُمُرِ، وَأَعُوذُ بِكَ مِنْ فِتْنَةِ الدُّنْيَا وَعَذَابِ القَبْرِ

Allahumma inni a'udhu bika minal bukhl, wa a'udhu bika minaljubn, wa a'udhu bika min an oradda ila ardhalil umur, wa a'udhu bika min fitnatid dunya wadhabil qabr

'O Allah, I take refuge in You from miserliness and cowardice, I take refuge in You lest I be returned to the worst of lives "i.e. old age, being weak, incapable and in a state of fear", and I take refuge in You from the trials and tribulations of this life and the punishment of the grave'

(61)

اللَّهُمَّ إِنِّي أَسْأَلُكَ الجَنَّةَ وأعوذُ بِكَ مِنَ النار

Allahumma inni as'alukal jannah,

wa a'udhu bika minannar

'O Allah, I ask You to grant me Paradise and I take refuge in You from the Fire'

(62)

اللَّهُمَّ بِعِلْمِكَ الغَيْبَ وَقُدْرَتِكَ عَلَى الخَلْقِ أَحْيِنِي ما عَلِمْتَ الحَياةَ خَيْراً لي، وَتَوَفَّنِي إذا عَلِمْتَ الوَفاةَ خَيْراً لي، اللَّهُمَّ إِنِّي أَسْأَلُكَ خَشْيَتَكَ في الغَيْبِ وَالشَّهادَةِ، وَأَسْأَلُكَ كَلِمَةَ الحَقِّ في الرِّضا وَالغَضَبِ، وَأَسْأَلُكَ القَصْدَ في الغِنى وَالفَقْرِ، وَأَسْأَلُكَ نَعِيماً لا يَنْفَدُ، وَأَسْأَلُكَ قُرَّةَ عَيْنٍ لا تَنْقَطِعُ وَأَسْأَلُكَ الرِّضا بَعْدَ القَضاءِ، وَأَسْأَلُكَ بَرْدَ العَيْشِ بَعْدَ المَوْتِ، وَأَسْأَلُكَ لَذَّةَ النَّظَرِ إلى وَجْهِكَ وَالشَّوْقَ إلى لِقائِكَ، في غَيْرِ ضَرَّاءَ مُضِرَّةٍ، وَلا فِتْنَةٍ مُضِلَّةٍ، اللَّهُمَّ زَيِّنا بِزِينَةِ الإيمانِ، وَاجْعَلْنا هُداةً مُهْتَدين

Allahumma bi'ilmikal ghayb, waqudratika alalkhalq, ahyini ma 'alimtal hayata khayran li wa tawaffani idha 'alimtal wafata khayran li, allahumma inni as'aluka khashyataka filghaybi washshahadah, wa as'aluka kalimatal haqqi firrida walghadab, waas'alukal qasda filghina walfaqr, wa as'aluka naeman la yanfad, wa as'aluka qurrata aynin la tanqati', wa as'alukarrida badalqad'a, wa as'aluka bardal 'ayshi b'adal mawt, waas'aluka ladhdhatan nadhari ila wajhik, wash shawqa ila liqaik fi ghayri darra mudirrah, wala fitnatin mudillah, allahumma zayyinna bizenatil iman waj'alna hudatan muhtadeen

'O Allah, by Your knowledge of the unseen and Your power over creation, keep me alive so long as You know such life to be good for me and take me if You know death to be better for me O Allah, make me fearful of You whether in secret or in public and I ask You to make me true in speech, in times of pleasure and anger I ask you to make me moderate in times of wealth and poverty and I ask You for everlasting bliss and joy which will never cease I ask You to make me pleased with what You have decreed and for an easy life after death I ask You for the sweetness of looking upon Your Face and a longing to encounter You in a manner which does not entail a calamity which will bring about harm nor a trial which will cause deviation O Allah, beautify us with the adornment of faith and make us of those who guide and are rightly guided'

(63)

اللّهُـمَّ إِنِّي أَسْأَلُكَ يا اللهُ بِأَنَّكَ الواحِدُ الأَحَد،الصَّمَدُ الَّذي لَـمْ يَلِـدْ وَلَمْ يولَد، وَلَمْ يَكُـنْ لَهُ كُفُواً أَحَد، أَنْ تَغْـفِرْ لي ذُنوبي إِنَّـكَ أَنْـتَ الغَفورُ الرَّحـيم

Allahumma inni as'aluka ya Allah biannakal wahidul ahadus samad, alladhi lam yalid walam yulad, walam

yakun lahu kufuwan ahad, an taghfira li dhunube innaka antal ghaforur raheem

'O Allah, I ask You O Allah, as You are The One, The Only, *as-Samad*, The One who begets not, nor was He begotten and there is none like unto Him that You forgive me my sins for verily You are The Oft Forgiving, Most Merciful'

as-Samad: The Self Sufficient Master, Possessor of perfect attributes whom all of creation turn to in all their needs

(64)

اللَّهُمَّ إِنِّي أَسْأَلُكَ بِأَنَّ لَكَ الْحَمْدُ لا إِلهَ إِلاّ أَنْتَ وَحْدَكَ لا شَرِيكَ لَكَ الْمَنَّانُ يا بَدِيعَ السَّمواتِ وَالأَرْضِ يا ذَا الْجَلالِ وَالإِكْرامِ، يا حَيُّ يا قَيُّومُ إِنِّي أَسْأَلُكَ الْجَنَّةَ وَأَعُوذُ بِكَ مِنَ النّارِ

Allahumma inni as'aluka bi'anna lakal hamd, la ilaha illa ant wahdaka la sharika lak, almannan, ya bade'as samawati wal ard, ya dhaljalali walikram, ya hayyu ya qayyom, inni as'alukal jannah, wa a'udhu bika minannar

'O Allah, I ask You as unto You is all praise, none has the right to be worshipped except You, alone, without partner You are the Benefactor O Originator of the heavens and the Earth, O Possessor of majesty and honour, O Ever Living, O Self Subsisting and Supporter of all, verily I ask You for Paradise and I take refuge with You from the Fire'

(65)

اللَّهُمَّ إِنِّي أَسْأَلُكَ بِأَنِّي أَشْهَدُ أَنَّكَ أَنْتَ اللَّهُ لا إِلهَ إِلَّا أَنْتَ، الأَحَدُ الصَّمَدُ الَّذِي لَمْ يَلِدْ وَلَمْ يُولَدْ، وَلَمْ يَكُنْ لَهُ كُفُواً أَحَد

Allahumma inni as'aluka bi'anni ashhadu annaka antallah, la ilaha illa ant, al'ahadus samad, alladhi lam yalid walam yulad walam yakun lahu kufuwan ahad

'O Allah, I ask You, as I bear witness that You are Allah, none has the right to be worshipped except You, The One, *as-Samad* Who begets not nor was He begotten and there is none like unto Him'

as-Samad: The Self Sufficient Master, Possessor of perfect attributes whom all of creation turn to in all their needs

25. Remembrance after salam

(66)

أَسْتَغْفِرُ اللَّه (ثلاثا)
اللَّهُمَّ أَنْتَ السَّلامُ، وَمِنْكَ السَّلامُ، تَبَارَكْتَ يَا ذَا الجَلالِ وَالإِكْرَام

Astaghfirullah (three times)
Allahumma antas salam waminkas salam, tabarakta ya dhaljalali wal ikram

'I ask Allah for forgiveness' (three times)
'O Allah, You are *as-Salam* and from You is all

peace, blessed are You, O Possessor of majesty and honour'

as-Salam: The One Who is free from all defects and deficiencies

(67)

لا إلهَ إلا اللَّهُ وحدَهُ لا شريكَ له، لهُ المُـلْكُ ولهُ الحَمْد، وهوَ على كلّ شَيءٍ قَدير، اللّهُـمَّ لا مانِعَ لِما أَعطَـيْت، وَلا مُعطِـيَ لِما مَنَـعْت، وَلا يَنْفَـعُ ذا الجَدِّ مِنْكَ الجَد

La ilaha illallahu wahdahu la sharika lah, lahulmulku walahulhamd, wahuwa 'ala kulli shay'in qadir, allahumma la mani'a lima a'tayt, wala m'utiya lima mana't, wala yanfa'u dhaljaddi minkaljad

'None has the right to be worshipped except Allah, alone, without partner, to Him belongs all sovereignty and praise and He is over all things omnipotent. O Allah, none can prevent what You have willed to bestow and none can bestow what You have willed to prevent, and no wealth or majesty can benefit anyone, as from You is all wealth and majesty'

(68)

لا إلهَ إلاّ اللّه، وحدَهُ لا شَريكَ له، لهُ الملكُ ولهُ الحَمد، وهوَ على كلّ شيءٍ قدير، لا حَـوْلَ وَلا قـوَّةَ إلاّ بِاللّه، لا إلهَ إلاّ اللّـه، وَلا نَعْبُـدُ إلاّ إيّـاه، لهُ النّعْـمَةُ وَلَهُ الفَضْلُ وَلَهُ الثّنـاءُ الحَسَن، لا

إلهَ إلا اللهُ مخلِصِينَ لَـهُ الدِّينَ وَلَوْ كَرِهَ الكافِرون

La ilaha illallah, wahdahu la sharika lah, lahul mulku walahul hamd, wahuwa 'ala kulli shay'in qadir la hawla wala quwwata illa billah, la ilaha illallah, wala n'abudu illa iyyah, lahun ni'matu walahul fadl walahuth thanaol hasan, la ilaha illallah mukhlisena lahudden walaw karihal kafiron

'None has the right to be worshipped except Allah, alone, without partner, to Him belongs all sovereignty and praise and He is over all things omnipotent There is no might nor power except with Allah, none has the right to be worshipped except Allah and we worship none except Him For Him is all favour, grace, and glorious praise None has the right to be worshipped except Allah and we are sincere in faith and devotion to Him although the disbelievers detest it'

(69)

سُبْحانَ اللهِ، والحَمْدُ لله، واللهُ أَكْبَر (ثلاثاً وثلاثين)

لا إلهَ إلاّ اللهُ وَحْدَهُ لا شريكَ لهُ، لهُ المُلكُ ولهُ الحَمْدُ، وهُوَ على كُلِّ شيءٍ قَدير

Subhanallah walhamdu lillah, wallahu akbar

(thirty three times)

La ilaha illallahu wahdahu la sharika lah, lahul mulku walahul hamd, wahuwa 'ala kulli shay'in qadir

'How perfect Allah is, all praise is for Allah, and

Allah is the greatest'
(thirty three times)

'None has the right to be worshipped except Allah, alone, without partner, to Him belongs all sovereignty and praise and He is over all things omnipotent'

(70)

The following three chapters should be recited once after *Dhuhr*, *Asr* and *Isha* prayers and thrice after *Fajr* and *Maghrib*

﴿قُلْ هُوَ اللَّهُ أَحَدٌ...﴾ [الإِخْلاصْ]
{Qul huwa Allahu ahad...} [al-Ikhlas]

﴿قُلْ أَعُوذُ بِرَبِّ الْفَلَقِ...﴾ [الفَلَقْ]
{Qul a'udhu birabbi alfalaq...} [al-Falaq]

﴿قُلْ أَعُوذُ بِرَبِّ النَّاسِ...﴾ [النَّاسْ]
{Qul a'udhu birabbi alnnas...} [an-Nas]

(71)

It is also from the sunnah to recite the verse of the Footstool (*Ayat al-Kursi*) after each prayer:

﴿اللهُ لا إله إلا هو الحي القيوم لا تأخذه سنة ولا نوم...﴾
{Allahu la ilaha illa huwa alhayyu alqayyomu la ta'khudhuhu sinatun wala nawm...}
[al-Baqarah: 255]

(72)

لا إلهَ إلاّ اللهُ وحْـدَهُ لا شريكَ له، لهُ المُلْكُ ولهُ الحَمْد، يُحيـي وَيُـمِـيتُ وهُوَ على كُلّ شيءٍ قدير (عَشر مَرّات بَعدَ المَغرب وَالصّبح)

La ilaha illallahu wahdahu la sharika lah, lahul mulku walahul hamd, yuhye wayumet, wahuwa 'ala kulli shay'in qadir

(ten times after the *maghrib* & *fajr* prayers)

'None has the right to be worshipped except Allah, alone, without partner, to Him belongs all sovereignty and praise, He gives life and causes death and He is over all things omnipotent'

(ten times after the *maghrib* and *fajr* prayers)

(73)

اللهُـمَّ إنِّـي أسْأَلُكَ عِلْمـاً نافِعـاً وَرِزْقـاً طَيِّبـاً، وَعَمَلاً مُتَقَبَّلاً (بَعْدَ السّلام مِن صَلاةِ الفَجْر)

Allahumma inni as'aluka ilman nafi'an, warizqan tayyiban, wa'amalan mutaqabbalan

(after salam from fajr prayer)

'O Allah, I ask You for knowledge which is beneficial and sustenance which is good, and deeds which are acceptable'

(To be said after giving salam for the fajr prayer)

26. Supplication for seeking guidance in forming a decision or choosing the proper course…etc (*al-Istikharah*)

(74)

On the authority of Jabir Ibn Abdullah ؓ, he said: 'The Prophet ﷺ would instruct us to pray for guidance in all of our concerns, just as he would teach us a chapter from the Quran He ﷺ would say 'If any of you intends to undertake a matter then let him pray two supererogatory units (two rakah nafilah) of prayer and after which he should supplicate:

اللَّهُمَّ إِنِّي أَسْتَخِيرُكَ بِعِلْمِكَ، وَأَسْتَقْدِرُكَ بِقُدْرَتِكَ، وَأَسْأَلُكَ مِنْ فَضْلِكَ الْعَظِيمِ، فَإِنَّكَ تَقْدِرُ وَلَا أَقْدِرُ، وَتَعْلَمُ وَلَا أَعْلَمُ، وَأَنْتَ عَلَّامُ الْغُيُوبِ، اللَّهُمَّ إِنْ كُنْتَ تَعْلَمُ أَنَّ هَذَا الْأَمْرَ - وَيُسَمِّي حَاجَتَهُ - خَيْرٌ لِي فِي دِينِي وَمَعَاشِي وَعَاقِبَةِ أَمْرِي، فَاقْدُرْهُ لِي وَيَسِّرْهُ لِي ثُمَّ بَارِكْ لِي فِيهِ، وَإِنْ كُنْتَ تَعْلَمُ أَنَّ هَذَا الْأَمْرَ شَرٌّ لِي فِي دِينِي وَمَعَاشِي وَعَاقِبَةِ أَمْرِي، فَاصْرِفْهُ وَاصْرِفْنِي عَنْهُ وَاقْدُرْ لِي الْخَيْرَ حَيْثُ كَانَ ثُمَّ أَرْضِنِي بِهِ

Allahumma inni astakheruka bi 'ilmik, wa astaqdiruka biqudratik, wa as'aluka min fadlikal adhim, fa innaka taqdiru wala aqdir, wat'alamu wala 'alam, wa anta 'allamul ghuyob, allahumma in kunta t'alamu anna hadhal amr (say your need) khayrun li fi dini wam'ashi wa 'aqibati amri faqdurhu li, wa yassirhu li, thumma barik li fih, wa'in kunta t'alamu anna hadhal amr

*sharrun li fi dini wama'she wa a'qibati amri fasrifhu
a'nni wasrifni a'nh, waqdur liyalkhayra haythu kan,
thumma ardini bih*

'O Allah, I seek Your counsel by Your knowledge
and by Your power I seek strength and I ask You
from Your immense favour, for verily You are
able while I am not and verily You know while
I do not and You are the Knower of the unseen.
O Allah, if You know this affair *and here you
mention your need* to be good for me in relation
to my religion, my life, and end, then decree
and facilitate it for me, and bless me with it, and
if You know this affair to be ill for me towards
my religion, my life, and end, then remove it
from me and remove me from it, and decree for
me what is good wherever it be and make me
satisfied with such'

One who seeks guidance from his Creator and
consults his fellow believers and then remains firm
in his resolve does not regret, for Allah has said:

﴿وَشَاوِرْهُـم فِي الأَمْرِ فَـإِذَا عَـزَمْتَ فَتَوَكَّـلْ عَلَى اللهِ﴾

*(wa shawirhum fi al amri faidha a'zamta fatawakkal
'ala Allah)*

(chapter 3 verse 159)

'...and consult them in the affair. Then when you
have taken a decision, put your trust in Allah...'

27. Remembrance said in the morning and evening

(as-Sabah) translated *morning*: after Fajr prayer until the sun rises, *(almasa/)* translated *evening*: after Asr prayer until the sunsets, however some scholars say: after the sunsets and onwards

(75)

In the evening:

أَمْسَيْنا وَأَمْسى المُلكُ لله وَالحَمدُ لله، لا إلهَ إلاَّ اللهُ وَحدَهُ لا شَريكَ لهُ، لهُ المُلكُ ولهُ الحَمْدُ، وهُوَ على كلِّ شَيءٍ قدير، رَبِّ أسْأَلُكَ خَيرَ ما في هـذهِ اللَّيْلةِ وخَيرَ ما بَعْدَها، وَأعوذُ بِكَ مِن شَرِّ هـذهِ اللَّيْلةِ وشَرِّ ما بَعْدَها، رَبِّ أعوذُبِكَ مِنَ الكَسَلِ وسوءِ الكِبَر، رَبِّ أعوذُبِكَ مِنْ عَذابٍ في النّارِ وَعَذابٍ في القَبْرِ.

Amsayna wa amsal mulku lillah wal hamdu lillah la ilaha illallah, wahdahu la sharika lah, lahul mulku walahul hamd, wahuwa 'ala kulli shay'in qadir, rabbi as'aluka khayra ma fi hadhihil laylah, wakhayra ma ba'daha, wa a'udhu bika min sharri hadhihil laylah, washarri ma ba'daha, rabbi a'udhu bika minal kasal, wa su'il kibar, rabbi a'udhu bika min adhabin finnar, wadhabin fil qabr

'We have reached the evening and at this very time unto Allah belongs all sovereignty, and all praise is for Allah None has the right to be worshipped except Allah, alone, without partner, to Him belongs all sovereignty and praise and He is over all things omnipotent My Lord, I ask You for the good of this night and the good of what follows it and I take refuge in You from the evil of this night and the evil of what follows it My Lord, I take refuge in You from laziness and senility My Lord, I take refuge in You from torment in the Fire and punishment in the grave'

...likewise, one says in the morning:

أَصْبَحْنا وَأَصْبَحَ المُلْكُ لله....

Asbahna wa asbahal mulku lillah...

'We have reached the morning and at this very time unto Allah belongs all sovereignty...'

(76)

اللَّهُمَّ بِكَ أَصْبَحْنا وَبِكَ أَمْسَيْنا،
وَبِكَ نَحْيا وَبِكَ نَموتُ وَإِلَيْكَ النُّشور.

Allahumma bika asbahna wabika amsayna, wabika nahya, wabika namotu wa ilaykan nushour

'O Allah, by your leave we have reached the morning and by Your leave we have reached the evening, by Your leave we live and die and unto You is our resurrection'

In the evening:

اللَّهُـمَّ بِكَ أَمْسَـيْنا، وَبِكَ أَصْبَحْنا،
وَبِكَ نَحْـيا، وَبِكَ نَـموتُ وَإِلَـيْكَ المَصير.

Allahumma bika amsayna, wabika asbahna, wabika nahya wabika namutu wailaykal maseer

'O Allah, by Your leave we have reached the evening and by Your leave we have reached the morning, by Your leave we live and die and unto You is our return'

(77)

اللَّهُمَّ أَنْتَ رَبِّي لا إلهَ إلاّ أَنْتَ، خَلَقْتَنِي وَأَنا عَبْدُكَ، وَأَنا عَلى عَهْدِكَ وَوَعْدِكَ ما اسْتَطَعْتُ، أَعوذُ بِكَ مِنْ شَرِّ ما صَنَعْتُ، أَبوءُ لَكَ بِنِعْمَتِكَ عَلَيَّ وَأَبوءُ بِذَنْبي فَاغْفِرْ لي فَإِنَّهُ لا يَغْفِرُ الذُّنوبَ إلاّ أَنْتَ

Allahumma anta rabbe la ilaha illa ant, khalaqtani wa ana a'bduk, wa ana 'ala ahdika wawa'dika matata't, a'udhu bika min sharri ma sana't, aboo' laka binimatika 'alay, waaboo' bidhanbi, faghfir li fainnahu la yaghfirudh dhunoba illa ant

'O Allah, You are my Lord, none has the right to be worshipped except You, You created me and I am Your servant and I abide to Your covenant and promise as best I can, I take refuge in You from the evil of which I have committed I acknowledge Your favour upon me and I acknowledge my sin, so forgive me, for verily none can forgive sin except You'

(78)

اللَّهُمَّ إِنِّي أَصْبَحْتُ أُشْهِدُكَ، وَأُشْهِدُ حَمَلَةَ عَرْشِكَ، وَمَلَائِكَتَكَ، وَجَمِيعَ خَلْقِكَ، أَنَّكَ أَنْتَ اللهُ لا إلهَ إلا أَنْتَ وَحْدَكَ لا شَرِيكَ لَكَ، وَأَنَّ مُحَمَّداً عَبْدُكَ وَرَسُولُكَ.

(أربع مرات حين يصبح أو يمسي)

Allahumma inni asbahtu oshhiduk, wa oshhidu hamalata a'rshik, wa malaikatak, wa jamea' khalqik, annaka antallahu la ilaha illa ant, wahdaka la sharika lak, wa anna Muhammadan 'abduka wa rasoluk

(four times in the morning & evening)

'O Allah, verily I have reached the morning and call on You, the bearers of Your throne, Your angles, and all of Your creation to witness that You are Allah, none has the right to be worshipped except You, alone, without partner and that Muhammad is Your Servant and Messenger'

(four times in the morning and evening)

Note: for the evening, one reads (*amsaytu*) instead of (*asbahtu*)

(79)

اللَّهُمَّ مَا أَصْبَحَ بِي مِنْ نِعْمَةٍ أَوْ بِأَحَدٍ مِنْ خَلْقِكَ، فَمِنْكَ وَحْدَكَ لا شَرِيكَ لَكَ، فَلَكَ الْحَمْدُ وَلَكَ الشُّكْرُ

Allahumma ma asbaha bi min ni'matin, aw bi'ahadin min khalqik, faminka wahdaka la sharika lak, falakal hamdu walakash shukr

'O Allah, what blessing I or any of Your creation have risen upon, is from You alone, without partner, so for You is all praise and unto You all thanks'

...whoever says this in the morning has indeed offered his day's thanks and whoever says this in the evening has indeed offered his night's thanks

Note: for the evening, one reads (*amsa*) instead of (*asbaha*)

(80)

اللَّهُمَّ عافِني في بَدَني، اللَّهُمَّ عافِني في سَمْعي، اللَّهُمَّ عافِني في بَصَري، لا إلهَ إلاّ أنْـتَ. (ثلاثاً)

اللَّهُمَّ إنّي أعـوذُبِكَ مِنَ الْكُـفر، وَالفَـقْر، وَأعـوذُبِكَ مِنْ عَذابِ القَبْرِ، لا إلهَ إلاّ أنْـتَ. (ثلاثاً)

Allahumma a'fini fi badani, allahumma a'fini fi sami', allahumma a'fini fi basari, la ilaha illa ant

(three times)

Allahumma inni a'udhu bika minal kufr, wal faqr, wa a'udhu bika min adhabil qabr, la ilaha illa ant

(three times)

'O Allah, grant my body health, O Allah, grant my hearing health, O Allah, grant my sight health None has the right to be worshipped except You'

(three times)

'O Allah, I take refuge with You from disbelief

and poverty, and I take refuge with You from the punishment of the grave None has the right to be worshipped except You' (three times)

(81)

حَسْبِيَ اللَّهُ لا إلهَ إلا هُوَ عَلَيْهِ تَوَكَّلْتُ وَهُوَ رَبُّ العَرْشِ العَظيم.

(سبع مَرات حين يصبح وَيمسي)

Hasbiyallahu la ilaha illa huwa, 'alayhi tawakkalt, wahuwa rabbul a'rshil adheem

(seven times morning & evening)

'Allah is Sufficient for me, none has the right to be worshipped except Him, upon Him I rely and He is Lord of the exalted throne'

(seven times morning and evening)

(82)

أَعوذُبِكَلِمـاتِ اللهِ التَّامـاتِ مِنْ شَرِّ ما خَلَق

(ثلاثاً إذا أمسى)

a'udhu bikalimatillahit tammati min sharri ma khalaq

(three times in the evening)

'I take refuge in Allah's perfect words from the evil He has created'

(three times in the evening)

(83)

اللَّهُمَّ إنِّي أَسْأَلُكَ العَفْوَ والعـافِـيَـةَ في الدُّنيا والآخِرَة، اللَّهُمَّ إنِّي أَسْأَلُكَ العَفْوَ والعـافِـيَـةَ في ديني وَدُنْيايَ وَأَهْلي وَمالي،

اللَّهُـمَّ اسْتُرْ عَوْراتِي وَآمِنْ رَوْعاتـي، اللَّهُمَّ احْفَظْنِي مِنْ بَيْنِ يَدَيَّ وَمِنْ خَلْفِي وَعَنْ يَـمِينِي وَعَنْ شِمـالِي، وَمِنْ فَوْقِي، وَأَعُوذُ بِعَظَمَتِكَ أَنْ أُغْتالَ مِنْ تَحْتِي

Allahumma inni as'alukal a'fwa wal a'fiyah, fiddunya wal akhirah, allahumma inni as'alukal a'fwa wal a'fiyah fi dini, wadunyaya wa ahli, wa mali, allahummastur a'wrati, waamin rawa'ti, allahummahfadhni min bayni yaday, wamin khalfi, wa'n yamini, wa'n shimali, wamin fawqi, wa a'udhu bia'zamatika an ughtala min tahti

'O Allah, I ask You for pardon and wellbeing
in this life and the next O Allah, I ask You
for pardon and wellbeing in my religious and
worldly affairs, and my family and my wealth
O Allah, veil my weaknesses and set at ease my
dismay O Allah, preserve me from the front and
from behind and on my right and on my left and
from above, and I take refuge with You lest I be
swallowed up by the earth'

(84)

اللَّهُمَّ عالِمَ الغَيْبِ وَالشَّهادَةِ فاطِرَ السَّماواتِ وَالأَرْضِ رَبَّ كُلِّ شَيْءٍ وَمَلِيكَهُ، أَشْهَدُ أَنْ لا إِلٰهَ إِلاَّ أَنْتَ، أَعُوذُ بِكَ مِنْ شَرِّ نَفْسِي وَمِنْ شَرِّ الشَّيْطانِ وَشِرْكِهِ، وَأَنْ أَقْتَرِفَ عَلَى نَفْسِي سُوءاً أَوْ أَجُرَّهُ إِلَى مُسْلِمٍ

Allahumma a'limal ghaybi wash shahadah, fatiras samawati wal ard, rabba kulli shay'in wa malikah, ashhadu an la ilaha illa ant, a'udhu bika min sharri

nafsi wamin sharrish shaytani wa shirkih, wan aqtarifa
'ala nafsi so'an aw ajurrahu ila muslim

'O Allah, Knower of the unseen and the seen, Creator of the heavens and the Earth, Lord and Sovereign of all things, I bear witness that none has the right to be worshipped except You I take refuge in You from the evil of my soul and from the evil and *shirk* of the devil, and from committing wrong against my soul or bringing such upon another Muslim'

shirk: to associate others with Allah in those things which are specific to Him This can occur in (1) belief, eg to believe that other than Allah has the power to benefit or harm, (2) speech, eg to swear by other than Allah and (3) action, eg to bow or prostrate to other than Allah

(85)

بِسْـمِ اللهِ الذي لا يَضُـرُّ مَعَ اسمِـهِ شَيءٌ فِي الأرْضِ وَلا فِي السَّماءِ وَهـوَ السَّميـعُ العَليـم (ثلاثاً)

Bismillahilladhi la yadurru ma'smihi shay'un filardi wala fissama'i wahuwas sami'ul aleem (three times)

'In the name of Allah with whose name nothing is harmed on earth nor in the heavens and He is The AllSeeing, The AllKnowing' (three times)

(86)

رَضِيتُ بِاللهِ رَبّاً وَبِالإِسْلامِ دِيناً وَبِمُحَمَّدٍ نَبِيّاً. (ثلاثا)

Raditu billahi rabban wabil islami dinan wabi
Muhammadin ﷺ nabiyya (three times)

'I am pleased with Allah as a Lord, and Islam as a religion and Muhammad ﷺ as a Prophet' (three times)

(87)

سُبْحَانَ اللهِ وَبِحَمْدِهِ عَدَدَ خَلْقِهِ، وَرِضَا نَفْسِهِ، وَزِنَةَ عَرْشِهِ، وَمِدَادَ كَلِمَاتِهِ. (ثلاثا)

Subhanallahi wabihamdih, 'adada khalqihi warida
nafsih, wazinata 'arshih, wamidada kalimatih
(three times)

'How perfect Allah is and I praise Him
by the number of His creation and His
pleasure, and by the weight of His throne,
and the ink of His words'
(three times)

(88)

سُبْحَانَ اللهِ وَبِحَمْدِهِ (مائة مرة)

Subhanallahi wabihamdih (one hundred times)

'How perfect Allah is and I praise Him'
(one hundred times)

(89)

يَا حَيُّ يَا قَيُّومُ بِرَحْمَتِكَ أَسْتَغِيثُ، أَصْلِحْ لِي شَأْنِي كُلَّهُ،

65

وَلا تَكِلـنِي إِلى نَفْسِي طَرْفَةَ عَين

Ya hayyu ya qayyum, birahmatika astagith, aslih li sh'ani kullah, wala takilni ila nafsi tarfata a'yn

'O Ever Living, O Self Subsisting and Supporter of all, by Your mercy I seek assistance, rectify for me all of my affairs and do not leave me to myself, even for the blink of an eye'

(90)

لا إلهَ إلاّ اللهُ وحْدَهُ لا شَـرِيكَ لهُ، لهُ المُـلْكُ ولهُ الحَمْـد، وهُوَ عَلى كُلّ شَيءٍ قَدِير. (مائة مرة)

La ilaha illallah, wahdahu la sharika lah, lahul mulku walahul hamd, wahuwa 'ala kulli shay'in qadir

(one hundred times)

'None has the right to be worshipped except Allah, alone, without partner, to Him belongs all sovereignty and praise, and He is over all things omnipotent'

(one hundred times every day)

(91)

أَصْبَحْـنا وَأَصْبَـحْ المُلْكُ لله رَبِّ العالَمـين، اللّهُـمَّ إِنِّي أَسْأَلُـكَ خَـيْرَ هذا اليَوْم، فَتْحَهُ، وَنَصْرَهُ، وَنورَهُ، وَبَرَكَتَهُ، وَهُداهُ، وَأَعـوذُ بِكَ مِنْ شَرِّ ما فيه وَشَرِّ ما بَعْدَه

Asbahna wa asbahal mulku lillahi rabbil 'alameen, allahumma inni as'aluka khayra hadhal yawm, fathahu, wanasrahu, wanurahu, wabarakatahu, wahudahu, wa a'udhu bika min sharri ma fihi, washarri ma ba'dah

'We have reached the morning and at this very time all sovereignty belongs to Allah, Lord of the worlds O Allah, I ask You for the good of this day, its triumphs and its victories, its light and its blessings and its guidance, and I take refuge in You from the evil of this day and the evil that follows it'

For the evening, the supplication is read as follows:

أَمْسَيْنا وَأَمْسى المُلْكُ لِلهِ رَبِّ العالَمـين، اللَّهُمَّ إِنِّي أَسْأَلُكَ خَيْرَ هـذه اللَّيْلَة، فَتْحَها، وَنَصْرَها، وَنورَها، وَبَرَكَتَها، وَهُداها، وَأَعـوذُ بِكَ مِنْ شَرِّ ما فيها وَشَرِّ ما بَعْدَها

Amsayna wa'amsal mulku lillahi rabbil 'alameen, allahumma inni as'aluka khayra hadhihil laylah, fathaha, wanasraha, wanuraha, wabarakataha, wahudaha, wa a'udhu bika min sharri ma fiha washarri ma ba'daha

'We have reached the evening and at this very time all sovereignty belongs to Allah, Lord of the worlds O Allah, I ask You for the good of tonight, its triumphs and its victories, its light and its blessings and its guidance, and I take refuge in You from the evil of tonight and the evil that follows it'

(92)

The messenger of Allah ﷺ said:
'Whoever says in the morning:

لا إلهَ إلاَّ اللهُ وحْـدَهُ لا شَريكَ لهُ، لهُ المُلْكُ ولهُ الحَمْد،

وهُوَ على كُلِّ شَيءٍ قَـدير

La ilaha illallahu wahdahu la sharika lah, lahul mulk, walahul hamd, wahuwa 'ala kulli shay'in qadir

'None has the right to be worshipped except Allah, alone, without partner, to Him belongs all sovereignty and praise and He is over all things omnipotent'

…has indeed gained the reward of freeing a slave from the children of Ismael, and ten of his sins are wiped away and he is raised ten degrees, and he has found a safe retreat from the devil until evening. Similarly, if he says it at evening time, he will be protected until the morning'

(93)

أَصْبَحْنا على فِطرَةِ الإسْلام، وَعَلى كَلِمَةِ الإخْلاص، وَعَلى دينِ نَبِيِّنا مُحَـمَّدٍ وَعَلى مِلَّةِ أبينا إبْراهيمَ حَنيفاً مُسْلِماً وَمـا كانَ مِنَ المُشْرِكين

asbahna 'ala fitratil islam, w'ala kalimatil ikhlas, w'ala dini nabiyyina Muhammad ﷺ w'ala millati abina Ibraheem, hanifan musliman wama kana minal mushrikeen

'We rise upon the *fitrah* of Islam, and the word of pure faith, and upon the religion of our Prophet Muhammad ﷺ and the religion of our forefather Ibrahem, who was a Muslim and of true faith and was not of those who associate others with Allah'

fitrah: state of purity, the way of Ibrahim
pure faith: the Shahada
Note: for the evening, one reads *amsayna* instead of *asbahna*

في المساء تستبدل كلمة أصبحنا بكلمة أمسينا

(94)
'Abdullah Ibn Khubaib ؓ said: 'The Messenger of Allah ﷺ said to me 'Recite!' I replied 'O Messenger of Allah, what shall I recite?' he said 'Recite:

﴿قُلْ هُوَ اللَّهُ أَحَدٌ...﴾ [الإخلاص]
{Qul huwa Allahu ahad...} [al-Ikhlas]

﴿قُلْ أَعُوذُ بِرَبِّ الفَلَقِ...﴾ [الفَلَق]
{Qul a'udhu birabbi alfalaq...} [al-Falaq]

﴿قُلْ أَعُوذُ بِرَبِّ النَّاسِ...﴾ [النَّاس]
{Qul a'udhu birabbi alnnas...} [an-Nas]

...in the evening and the morning three times for it will suffice you of all else'

28. Remembrance before sleeping

(95)
'When retiring to his bed every night, the Prophet ﷺ would hold his palms together, spit (A form of spitting comprising mainly of air with little spittle) in them, recite the last three

chapters (al-Ikhlas, al-Falaq, an-Nas) of the Quran and then wipe over his entire body as much as possible with his hands, beginning with his head and face and then all parts of the body, he would do this three times'

(96)

The Prophet ﷺ also said: 'When you are about to sleep recite ayatul kursi (The verse of the footstool, chapter 2:255) till the end of the verse for there will remain over you a protection from Allah and no devil will draw near to you until morning'

(97)

The Prophet ﷺ also said: *'Whoever recites the last two verses of Surat al-Baqarah at night, those two verses shall be sufficient for him (i.e. protect him from all that can cause him harm)'*

﴿آمَنَ الرَّسُولُ بِمَا أُنزِلَ إِلَيْهِ مِن رَّبِّهِ وَالْمُؤْمِنُونَ...﴾

(Amana arrasulu bima unzila ilayhi min rabbihi wa almu'minoona...)

[al-Baqarah: 285-286]

(98)

'If one of you rises from his bed and then returns to it he should dust it with the edge of his garment three times for he does not know what has occurred in his absence and when he lies down he should supplicate:

بِاسْمِكَ رَبِّي وَضَعْتُ جَنْبِي، وَبِكَ أَرْفَعُهُ، فَإِنْ أَمْسَكْتَ نَفْسِي فَارْحَمْهَا، وَإِنْ أَرْسَلْتَهَا فَاحْفَظْهَا بِمَا تَحْفَظُ بِهِ عِبَادَكَ الصَّالِحِيْنَ

Bismika rabbi wada'tu janbi wabika arfa'uh, fa'in amsakta nafsi farhamha, wa'in arsaltaha fahfadhha bima tahfazu bihi ibadakas saliheen

'In Your name my Lord, I lie down and in Your name I rise, so if You should take my soul then have mercy upon it, and if You should return my soul then protect it in the manner You do so with Your righteous servants'

(99)

اللَّهُمَّ إِنَّكَ خَلَقْتَ نَفْسِي وَأَنْتَ تَوَفَّاهَا لَكَ مَمَاتُهَا وَمَحْيَاهَا، إِنْ أَحْيَيْتَهَا فَاحْفَظْهَا، وَإِنْ أَمَتَّهَا فَاغْفِرْ لَهَا. اللَّهُمَّ إِنِّي أَسْأَلُكَ الْعَافِيَةَ

Allahumma innaka khalaqta nafsi wa anta tawaffaha, laka mamatuha wamahyaha in ahyaytaha fahfadhha, wa'in amattaha faghfir laha Allahumma inni as'alukal afiyah

'O Allah, verily You have created my soul and You shall take it's life, to You belongs it's life and death If You should keep my soul alive then protect it, and if You should take it's life then forgive it
O Allah, I ask You to grant me good health'

(100)

The Prophet ﷺ would place his right hand under his cheek when about to sleep and supplicate:

اللَّهُمَّ قِنِي عَذَابَكَ يَوْمَ تَبْعَثُ عِبَادَكَ. (ثَلاثًا)

Allahumma qini dhabaka yawma taba'thu ibadak

(three times)

'O Allah, protect me from Your punishment on the day Your servants are resurrected' (three times)

(101)

بِاسْمِكَ اللَّهُمَّ أَمُوتُ وَأَحْيَا

Bismikallahumma amutu wa ahya

'In Your name O Allah, I live and die'

(102)

'Shall I not direct you both (The Prophet ﷺ was addressing Ali and Fatimah may Allah be pleased with them when they approached him for a servant) to something better than a servant? When you go to bed say:

Subhanallah (thirtythree times)

سُبْحَانَ اللَّهِ (ثَلاثًا وَثَلاثِين)

'How Perfect Allah is' (thirtythree times)

Alhamdu lillah (thirtythree times)

الحَمْدُ لله (ثَلاثًا وَثَلاثِين)

'All praise is for Allah' (thirtythree times)

Allahu akbar (thirtyfour times)

اللَّهُ أَكْبَرُ (أَرْبَعًا وَثَلَاثِينَ)

'Allah is the greatest' (thirtyfour times)
...for that is indeed better for you both
than a servant'

(103)

اللَّهُمَّ رَبَّ السَّمَوَاتِ السَّبْعِ وَرَبَّ الْعَرْشِ الْعَظِيمِ، رَبَّنَا وَرَبَّ كُلِّ شَيْءٍ، فَالِقَ الْحَبِّ وَالنَّوَى، وَمُنَزِّلَ التَّوْرَاةِ وَالإِنْجِيلِ، وَالْفُرْقَانِ، أَعُوذُ بِكَ مِنْ شَرِّ كُلِّ شَيْءٍ أَنْتَ آخِذٌ بِنَاصِيَتِهِ. اللَّهُمَّ أَنْتَ الأَوَّلُ فَلَيْسَ قَبْلَكَ شَيْءٌ، وَأَنْتَ الآخِرُ فَلَيْسَ بَعْدَكَ شَيْءٌ، وَأَنْتَ الظَّاهِرُ فَلَيْسَ فَوْقَكَ شَيْءٌ، وَأَنْتَ الْبَاطِنُ فَلَيْسَ دُونَكَ شَيْءٌ، اقْضِ عَنَّا الدَّيْنَ وَأَغْنِنَا مِنَ الْفَقْرِ

*Allahumma rabbas samawatissab', warabbal
a'rshil adhim, rabbana warabba kulli shay', faliqal
habbi wannawa, wamunazzilat tawra, walinjel,
walfurqan, a'udhu bika min sharri kulli shay'in anta
akhidhun binasiyatih allahumma antalawwal, falaysa
qablaka shay', waantal akhir, falaysa ba'daka shay',
waantaddhahir falaysa fawqaka shay', wantal batin,
falaysa donaka shay', iqdi annad dayna waaghnina
minal faqr*

'O Allah, Lord of the seven heavens and the
exalted throne, our Lord and Lord of all things,
Splitter of the seed and the date stone, Revealer
of the *Tawrah* (Torah), the *Injil* (Bible) and the
Furqan (Quran), I take refuge in You from the
evil of all things You shall seize by the forelock

(i.e. You have total mastery over) O Allah, You are The First so there is nothing before You and You are The Last so there is nothing after You You are *at-Thahir* so there is nothing above You and You are *al-Batin* so there is nothing closer than You Settle our debt for us and spare us from poverty'

Tawrah: The book revealed to Moosa u
Injil: The book revealed to Easa u
Furqan: One of the many names of the Quran, means: The Criterion which distinguishes between truth and falsehood
at-Thahir: Indicates the greatness of His attributes and the insignificance of every single creation in respect to His greatness and Highness, for He is above all of His creation as regards His essence and attributes
al-Batin: Indicates His awareness and knowledge of all secrets, of that which is in the hearts and the most intimate of things just as it indicates His closeness and nearness to all in a manner which befits His majesty

(104)

الحَمْدُ لله الَّذِي أَطْعَمَنَا وَسَقَانَا، وَكَفَانَا، وَآوَانَا،
فَكَمْ مِمَّنْ لا كَافِيَ لَهُ وَلا مُؤْوِي

Alhamdu lillahilladhi at'amana wasaqana, wakafana,

wa awana, fakam mimman la kafiya lahu wala mu'we

'All praise is for Allah, Who fed us and gave us drink, and Who is sufficient for us and has sheltered us, for how many have none to suffice them or shelter them'

(105)

اللَّهُمَّ عَالِمَ الْغَيْبِ وَالشَّهَادَةِ فَاطِرَ السَّمَاوَاتِ وَالأَرْضِ رَبَّ كُلِّ شَيْءٍ وَمَلِيكَهُ، أَشْهَدُ أَنْ لا إِلَهَ إِلاَّ أَنْتَ، أَعُوذُ بِكَ مِنْ شَرِّ نَفْسِي، وَمِنْ شَرِّ الشَّيْطَانِ وَشِرْكِهِ، وَأَنْ أَقْتَرِفَ عَلَى نَفْسِي سُوءاً أَوْ أَجُرَّهُ إِلَى مُسْلِم

Allahumma alimal ghaybi wash shahadah, fatiras samawati wal ard, rabba kulli shay'in wamalekah, ashhadu an la ilaha illa ant, a'udhu bika min sharri nafsi wamin sharrish shaytani washirkih, wa an aqtarifa 'ala nafsi sooan aw ajurrahu ila muslim

'O Allah, Knower of the seen and the unseen, Creator of the heavens and the earth, Lord and Sovereign of all things I bear witness that none has the right to be worshipped except You I take refuge in You from the evil of my soul and from the evil and *shirk* of the devil, and from committing wrong against my soul or bringing such upon another Muslim'

shirk: to associate others with Allah in those things which are specific to Him This can occur in (1) belief, eg to believe that other than Allah has the power to benefit or harm, (2) speech, eg to swear by other than Allah and (3) action, eg to bow or prostrate to other than Allah

(106)

'The Prophet ﷺ never used to sleep until he had recited Surat as-Sajdah (chapter 32) and Surat al-Mulk (chapter 67)'

(107)

'If you take to your bed, then perform ablution, lie on your right side and then supplicate:

اللَّهُمَّ أَسْلَمْتُ نَفْسِي إِلَيْكَ، وَفَوَّضْتُ أَمْرِي إِلَيْكَ، وَوَجَّهْتُ وَجْهِي إِلَيْكَ، وَأَلْجَأْتُ ظَهْرِي إِلَيْكَ، رَغْبَةً وَرَهْبَةً إِلَيْكَ، لا مَلْجَأَ وَلا مَنْجَا مِنْكَ إِلاَّ إِلَيْكَ، آمَنْتُ بِكِتَابِكَ الَّذِي أَنْزَلْتَ وَبِنَبِيِّكَ الَّذِي أَرْسَلْتَ

Allahumma aslamtu nafsi ilayk, wafawwadtu amri ilayk, wa wajjahtu wajhe ilayk, wa alja'tu dhahri ilayk, raghbatan warahbatan ilayk, la malja' wala manja minka illa ilayk, amantu bikitabik alladhi anzalt, wa binabiyyik alladhi arsalt

'O Allah, I submit my soul unto You, and I entrust my affair unto You, and I turn my face towards You, and I totally rely on You, in hope and fear of You Verily there is no refuge nor safe haven from You except with You I believe in Your Book which You have revealed and in Your

Prophet whom You have sent'
...If you then die, you will die upon the fitrah'

fitrah: state of purity, the way of Ibrahim

29. Supplication when turning over during the night

(108)

'Aisha ؓ narrated that the Messenger of Allah ﷺ used to say at night if he turned during sleep:

لَا إِلَهَ إِلَّا اللَّهُ الوَاحِدُ القَهَّارُ، رَبُّ السَّمَوَاتِ وَالأَرْضِ وَمَا بَيْنَهُمَا، العَزِيْزُ الغَفَّارُ

La ilaha illallahul wahidul qahhar, rabbus samawati wama baynahuma, alazezul ghaffar

'None has the right to be worshipped except Allah, The One, *ALQahhar*Lord of the heavens and the Earth and all between them, The Exalted in Might, The OftForgiving'

al-Qahhar: The One Who has subdued all of creation and Whom all of creation are subservient to All movements occur by His will

30. Upon experiencing unrest, fear, apprehensiveness and the like during sleep

(109)

أَعُوذُ بِكَلِمَاتِ اللَّهِ التَّامَّاتِ مِنْ غَضَبِهِ وَعِقَابِهِ، وَشَرِّ عِبَادِهِ وَمِنْ هَمَزَاتِ الشَّيَاطِينِ وَأَنْ يَحْضُرُونَ.

a'udhu bikalimatil lahittammat min ghadabih, wa 'iqabih, washarri ibadih, wamin hamazatish shayateen, wa an yahduron

'I take refuge in the perfect words of Allah from His anger and punishment, and from the evil of His servants, and from the madness and appearance of devils'

31. Upon seeing a good dream or a bad dream

(110)

'The righteous dream is from Allah and the bad dream is from the devil, so if anyone sees something which pleases him then he should only relate it to one whom he loves...'
Summary of what to do upon having a bad dream:
- Spit on your left three times

Spit: A form of spitting comprising mainly of air with little spittle
- Seek refuge in Allah from shaytan and the evil

of what you saw
- Do not relate it to anyone
- Turn and sleep on the opposite side to which you were sleeping on previously

(111)
- Get up and pray if you so desire

32. Qunoot al-Witr

al-Witr: Supplication made before or after bowing in the witr prayer

(112)

اللَّهُمَّ اهْدِنِي فِيمَنْ هَدَيْتَ، وَعَافِنِي فِيمَنْ عَافَيْتَ، وَتَوَلَّنِي فِيمَنْ تَوَلَّيْتَ، وَبَارِكْ لِي فِيمَا أَعْطَيْتَ، وَقِنِي شَرَّ مَا قَضَيْتَ، فَإِنَّكَ تَقْضِي وَلَا يُقْضَى عَلَيْكَ، إِنَّهُ لَا يَذِلُّ مَنْ وَالَيْتَ، [وَلَا يَعِزُّ مَنْ عَادَيْتَ]، تَبَارَكْتَ رَبَّنَا وَتَعَالَيْتَ.

Allahummahdini fiman hadayt, w'afini feman 'afayt, watawallani fiman tawallayt, wabarik li fima atayt, waqini sharra ma qadayt, fa'innaka taqdi wala yuqda 'alayk, innahu la yadhillu man walayt, [wala ya'izzu man 'adayt], tabarakta rabbana wat'alayt

'O Allah, guide me along with those whom You have guided, pardon me along with those whom You have pardoned, be an ally to me along with those whom You are an ally to and bless for me that which You have bestowed Protect me from the evil You have decreed for verily You decree and none can decree over You For surety, he whom you show allegiance to is never abased and he whom You take as an enemy is never honoured and mighty O our Lord, Blessed and Exalted are You'

Evil you have decreed: Allah does not create pure evil which does not have any good or contain any benefit, wisdom or mercy at all, nor does He punish anyone without having committed a sin Something can be good in terms of its creation when viewed in a particular perspective and at the same time be evil when viewed in another way Allah created the devil and by him, He tests His servants, so there are those who hate the devil, fight him and his way and they stand at enmity towards him and his followers and there are others who are at allegiance with the devil and follow his steps So evil exists in His creatures by His will and wisdom, not in His actions or act of creating

(113)

اللَّهُمَّ إِنِّي أَعُوذُ بِرِضَاكَ مِنْ سَخَطِكَ، وَبِمُعَافَاتِكَ مِنْ عُقُوبَتِكَ، وَأَعُوذُ بِكَ مِنْكَ، لَا أُحْصِي ثَنَاءً عَلَيْكَ، أَنْتَ كَمَا أَثْنَيْتَ عَلَى نَفْسِكَ

*Allahumma inni a'udhu biridaka min sakhatik,
wabimu'afatika min 'uqobatik, wa a'udhu bika mink, la
ohse thana'an 'alayk, anta kama athnayta 'ala nafsik*

'O Allah, I take refuge within Your pleasure from
Your displeasure and within Your pardon from
Your punishment, and I take refuge in You from
You I cannot enumerate Your praise You are as
You have praised Yourself'

(114)

اللَّهُمَّ إِيَّاكَ نَعْبُدُ، وَلَكَ نُصَلِّي وَنَسْجُدُ، وَإِلَيْكَ نَسْعَى وَنَحْفِدُ، نَرْجُو رَحْمَتَكَ، وَنَخْشَى عَذَابَكَ، إِنَّ عَذَابَكَ بِالْكَافِرِيْنَ مُلْحَقٌ. اللَّهُمَّ إِنَّا نَسْتَعِيْنُكَ وَنَسْتَغْفِرُكَ، وَنُثْنِي عَلَيْكَ الْخَيْرَ، وَلَا نَكْفُرُكَ، وَنُؤْمِنُ بِكَ، وَنَخْضَعُ لَكَ وَنَخْلَعُ مَنْ يَكْفُرُكَ

*Allahumma iyyaka n'abud, walaka nusalle wanasjud,
wa'ilayka nas'a wanahfid, narjo rahmatak, wa
nakhsha adhabak, inna adhabaka bilkafirena mulhaq
Allahumma inna nasta'enuk, wanastaghfiruk, wanuthni
'alaykal khayr, wala nakfuruk, wanu'minu bik,
wanakhdau lak wanakhl'au man yakfuruk*

'O Allah, it is You we worship, and unto You we
pray and prostrate, and towards You we hasten
and You we serve We hope for Your mercy and
fear Your punishment, verily Your punishment
will fall upon the disbelievers O Allah, we seek
Your aid and ask Your pardon, we praise You
with all good and do not disbelieve in You We

believe in You and submit unto You, and we disown and reject those who disbelieve in You

33. Remembrance immediately after salam of the witr prayer

(115)

The Messenger of Allah ﷺ would recite (the following chapters) during the witr prayer:

(Sabbi hisma rabbikal 'ala ......)

﴿سَبِّحِ اسْمَ رَبِّكَ الأَعْلَى...﴾

[Alala]

(Qul ya ayyuhal kafirun ......)

﴿قُلْ يَا أَيُّهَا الْكَافِرُونَ...﴾

[al-Kafirun]

(Qul huwa Allahu ahad ....)

﴿قُلْ هُوَ اللَّهُ أَحَدٌ...﴾

[al-Ikhlas]

......after giving salam he would supplicate three times:

سُبْحَانَ الْمَلِكِ الْقُدُّوسِ (ثَلَاثَ مَرَّاتٍ)

Subhanal malikil quddus (three times)

'How perfect The King, The Holy One is' (three times)

......on the third time he would raise his voice, elongate it and add:

Rabbil mala'ikati warruh

رَبِّ الْمَلَائِكَةِ وَالرُّوحِ

'Lord of the angles and the Ruh (i.e. Jibrael)

34. Supplication for anxiety and sorrow

(116)

اللَّهُمَّ إِنِّي عَبْدُكَ ابْنُ عَبْدِكَ ابْنُ أَمَتِكَ نَاصِيَتِي بِيَدِكَ، مَاضٍ فِيَّ حُكْمُكَ، عَدْلٌ فِيَّ قَضَاؤُكَ أَسْأَلُكَ بِكُلِّ اسْمٍ هُوَ لَكَ سَمَّيْتَ بِهِ نَفْسَكَ أَوْ أَنْزَلْتَهُ فِي كِتَابِكَ، أَوْ عَلَّمْتَهُ أَحَدًا مِنْ خَلْقِكَ أَوِ اسْتَأْثَرْتَ بِهِ فِي عِلْمِ الْغَيْبِ عِنْدَكَ أَنْ تَجْعَلَ الْقُرْآنَ رَبِيعَ قَلْبِي، وَنُورَ صَدْرِي وَجَلَاءَ حُزْنِي وَذَهَابَ هَمِّي

*Allahumma inni 'abduk, ibnu 'abdik, ibnu amatik,
nasiyate biyadik, madin fiyya hukmuk, adlun fiyya
qada'uk, as'aluka bikulli ismin huwa lak, sammayta bihi
nafsak, aw anzaltahu fi kitabik, aw 'allamtahu ahadan
min khalqik awista'tharta bihi fi ilmil ghaybi 'indak, an
taj'alal qur'ana rabi'a qalbi, wanura sadri, wajala' huzni
wadhahaba hammi*

'O Allah, I am Your servant, son of Your servant, son of Your maidservant, my forelock is in Your hand (i.e. You have total mastery over), Your command over me is forever executed and Your decree over me is just I ask You by every name belonging to You which You named Yourself with, or revealed in Your Book, or You taught to any of Your creation, or You have preserved in the knowledge of the unseen with You, that You make the Quran the life of my heart and the

light of my breast, and a departure for my sorrow
and a release for my anxiety'

(117)

اللَّهُمَّ إِنِّي أَعُوذُ بِكَ مِنَ الهَمِّ وَالحُزْنِ، وَالعَجْزِ وَالكَسَلِ وَالبُخْلِ وَالجُبْنِ، وَضَلَعِ الدَّيْنِ وَغَلَبَةِ الرِّجَالِ

Allahumma inni a'udhu bika minal hammi wal huzn, wal'ajzi walkasali walbukhli waljubn, wadal'id dayni waghalabatir rijal

'O Allah, I take refuge in You from anxiety and sorrow, weakness and laziness, miserliness and cowardice, the burden of debts and from being over powered by men'

35. Supplication for one in distress

(118)

لا إِلَهَ إِلاَّ اللهُ العَظِيْمُ الحَلِيْمُ، لا إِلَهَ إِلاَّ اللهُ رَبُّ العَرْشِ العَظِيْمِ، لا إِلَهَ إِلاَّ اللهُ رَبُّ السَّمَوَاتِ وَرَبُّ الأَرْضِ وَرَبُّ العَرْشِ الكَرِيْمِ

La ilaha illallahul 'adhimul haleem, la ilaha illallahu rabbul 'arshil 'adhim, la ilaha illallahu rabbus samawati wa rabbul ardi wa rabbul 'arshil kareem

'None has the right to be worshipped except Allah Forbearing None has the right to be worshipped except Allah, Lord of the magnificent throne None has the right to be worshipped except Allah, Lord of the heavens,

Lord of the Earth and Lord of the noble throne'

(119)

اللَّهُمَّ رَحْمَتَكَ أَرْجُو فَلا تَكِلْنِي إِلَى نَفْسِي طَرْفَةَ عَيْنٍ، وَأَصْلِحْ لِي شَأْنِي كُلَّهُ لا إِلَهَ إِلاَّ أَنْتَ.

Allahumma rahmataka arju fala takilni ila nafsi tarfata 'ayn, wa aslih li sh'ani kullah, la ilaha illa ant

'O Allah, it is Your mercy that I hope for, so do not leave me in charge of my affairs even for a blink of an eye and rectify for me all of my affairs None has the right to be worshipped except You'

(120)

لا إِلَهَ إِلاَّ أَنْتَ سُبْحَانَكَ إِنِّي كُنْتُ مِنَ الظَّالِمِينَ

La ilaha illa anta subhanaka inni kuntu minaz dhalimeen

'None has the right to be worshipped except You How perfect You are, verily I was among the wrongdoers'

(121)

اللهُ اللهُ رَبِّ لا أُشْرِكُ بِهِ شَيْئاً

Allahu Allahu rabbi la ushrika bihi shay'a

'Allah, Allah is my Lord, I do not associate anything with Him'

36. Upon encountering an enemy or those of authority

(122)

اللَّهُمَّ إِنَّا نَجْعَلُكَ فِي نُحُورِهِمْ، وَنَعُوذُ بِكَ مِنْ شُرُورِهِمْ

Allahumma inna naj'aluka fi nuhurihim wana'udhu bika min shururihim

'O Allah, we place You before them and we take refuge in You from their evil'

(123)

اللَّهُمَّ أَنْتَ عَضُدِي، وَأَنْتَ نَصِيرِي، بِكَ أَجُولُ وَبِكَ أَصُولُ وَبِكَ أُقَاتِلُ

Allahumma anta 'adudi, wa anta naseri, bika ajulu wa bika asulu wabika uqatilu

'O Allah, You are my supporter and You are my helper, by You I move and by You I attack and by You I battle'

(124)

حَسْبُنَا اللهُ وَنِعْمَ الوَكِيلُ

Hasbunallahu wani'mal wakeel

'Allah is sufficient for us, and how fine a trustee (He is)'

37. Supplication for one afflicted with doubt in his faith

(125)

- He should seek refuge in Allah
- He should renounce that which is causing such doubt

(126)

- He should say:

آمَنْتُ بِاللهِ وَرُسُلِهِ

Amantu billahi wa rusulih

'I have believed in Allah and His Messenger'

(127)

- He should also recite the following verse:

﴿هُوَ الأَوَّلُ وَالآخِرُ وَالظَّاهِرُ وَالبَاطِنُ وَهُوَ بِكُلِّ شَيْءٍ عَلِيمٌ﴾

(Huwa awwalu, wal akhiru, wa dhahiru wal batinu wahuwa bikulli shay'in 'aleem)

'He is The First and The Last, *at-Thahir* and *al-Batin* and He knows well all things'

At Thahir: Indicates the greatness of His attributes and the insignificance of every single creation in respect to His greatness and Highness, for He is above all of His creation as regards His essence and attributes

al-Batin: Indicates His awareness and knowledge of all secrets, of that which is in the hearts and the most intimate of things just as it indicates His closeness and nearness to all in a manner which befits His majesty

38. Settling a debt

(128)

اللَّهُمَّ اكْفِنِي بِحَلَالِكَ عَنْ حَرَامِكَ، وَأَغْنِنِي بِفَضْلِكَ عَمَّنْ سِوَاكَ

Allahummakfini bihalalika 'an haramik, wa aghnini bifadlika 'amman siwak

'O Allah, make what is lawful enough for me, as opposed to what is unlawful, and spare me by Your grace, of need of others'

(129)

اللَّهُمَّ إِنِّي أَعُوذُ بِكَ مِنَ الْهَمِّ وَالْحُزْنِ، وَالْعَجْزِ وَالْكَسَلِ وَالْبُخْلِ وَالْجُبْنِ، وَضَلَعِ الدَّيْنِ وَغَلَبَةِ الرِّجَالِ

Allahumma inni a'udhu bika minal hammi walhuzn, wal 'ajzi walkasal, walbukhl, waljubn, wadali'd dayni waghalabatir rijal

'O Allah, I take refuge in You from anxiety and sorrow, weakness and laziness, miserliness and cowardice, the burden of debts and from being over powered by men'

39. Supplication for one afflicted by whisperings in prayer or recitation

(130)

'Uthman Ibn Alas ﷺ narrated: I said 'O Messenger of Allah, verily the devil comes between me and my prayer and recitation making me confused' The Messenger of Allah ﷺ replied 'That is a devil called Khanzab, so if you sense his presence then seek refuge in Allah from him and spit (A form of spitting comprising mainly of air with little spittle) on your left side three times'

40. Supplication for one whose affairs have become difficult

(131)

اللّهُـمَّ لا سَـهْلَ إلاّ ما جَعَلـتَهُ سَهلاً، وَأَنْتَ تَجْعَلُ الْحَزَنَ إذا شِئْتَ سَهْلاً

Allahumma la sahla illa ma j'altahu sahla, wa anta taj'alul hazana idha shi'ta sahla

'O Allah, there is no ease except in that which You have made easy, and You make the difficulty, if You wish, easy'

41. Upon committing a sin

(132)
'Any servant who commits a sin and as a result, performs ablution, prays two units of prayer (i.e. two rakas) and then seeks Allah's forgiveness, Allah would forgive him'

42. Supplication for expelling the devil and his whisperings

(133)
- Seeking refuge from him

(134)
- The adhan (call to prayer)

(135)
- Recitation of the Quran and the authentic texts of remembrance and supplications *eg 'Do not make your homes like the graveyards, indeed the devils flee from the house in which soorat al-Baqarah has been read'* related by Muslim 1/539, also supplication and remembrance for the morning & evening, before sleep, when getting up, entering and leaving the toilet, entering and leaving the mosque, the

recitation of ayat Alkursiyy and the last two verses of soorat AlBaqarah before sleeping, the adhan……etc

43. Supplication when stricken with a mishap or overtaken by an affair

(136)

'The strong believer is better and more beloved to Allah, than the weak believer and there is goodness in both Strive for that which will benefit you, seek help from Allah and do not despair If a mishap should happen to befall you then do not say 'If only I had acted…such and such would have happened' Rather, say:

قَدَّرَ اللَّهُ وَمَا شَاءَ فَعَل

Qaddarallah, wama shaa'a fa'al

'Allah has decreed and what He wills, He does'
……for verily 'If' lets in the work of the devil'

(137)

Indeed Allah ﷻ rebukes due to negligence and slackness, but take to determination and caution, and if a matter should overtake you then say:

حَسْبِيَ اللَّهُ وَنِعْمَ الوَكِيْلُ

Hasbiyallah, wan'imal wakeel

'Allah is sufficient for me, and how fine a trustee

44. Placing children under Allah's protection

(138)
Ibn Abbas related that the Messenger of Allah ﷺ used to commend al-Hasan and al-Husayn to Allah's protection, saying:

أُعِيْذُكُمَا بِكَلِمَاتِ اللّهِ التَّامَّةِ، مِنْ كُلِّ شَيْطَانٍ وَهَامَّةٍ، وَمِنْ كُلِّ عَيْنٍ لاَمَّةٍ

U'idhukuma bikalimatillahit tammah, min kulli shaytanin wahammah, wamin kulli 'aynin lammah

'I commend you two to the protection of Allah's perfect words from every devil, vermin, and every evil eye'

45. When visiting the sick

(139)
When the Prophet ﷺ would enter upon a sick person, he would say:

لا بَأْسَ طَهُوْرٌ إِنْ شَاءَ الله

La ba'sa tahurun in sha' Allah

'Never mind, may it (the sickness) be a purification, if Allah wills'

(140)

'Any Muslim servant who visits a sick person whose prescribed moment of death has not arrived and supplicates seven times:

أَسْأَلُ اللَّهَ العَظِيْمَ، رَبَّ العَرْشِ العَظِيْمِ أَنْ يَشْفِيَكَ (سَبْعَ مَرَّات)

Asalullahal adhim rabbal 'arshil 'adhim an yashfeek

(seven times)

'I ask Allah The Supreme, Lord of the magnificent throne to cure you'

……he (the sick person) will be cured'

46. Excellence of visiting the sick

(141)

'Ali Ibn Abi Talib ؓ related that he heard the Messenger of Allah ﷺ say: 'If a man calls on his sick Muslim brother, it is as if he walks reaping the fruits of Paradise until he sits, and when he sits he is showered in mercy, and if this was in the morning, seventy thousand angles send prayers upon him until the evening, and if this was in the evening, seventy thousand angles send prayers upon him until the morning'

47. Supplication of the sick who have renounced all hope of life

(142)

اللّٰهُمَّ اغْفِرْ لِي وَارْحَمْنِي وَأَلْحِقْنِي بِالرَّفِيقِ الْأَعْلَى

Allahummaghfir li, warhamni waalhiqni birrafiqil 'ala

'O Allah, forgive me, have mercy upon me and unite me with the higher companions'

Refer to the Quran, chapter 4, verse: 69

(143)

Aishah related that the Prophet (during his illness in which he passed away) would dip his hands in water and then he would wipe his face and say:

لَا إِلَهَ إِلَّا اللَّهُ، إِنَّ لِلْمَوْتِ لَسَكَرَات

La ilaha illallah, inna lilmawti lasakarat

'None has the right to be worshipped except Allah, death does indeed contain agony'

(144)

لَا إِلَهَ إِلَّا اللَّهُ وَاللَّهُ أَكْبَرُ، لَا إِلَهَ إِلَّا اللَّهُ وَحْدَهُ لَا شَرِيكَ لَهُ، لَا إِلَهَ إِلَّا اللَّهُ لَهُ الْمُلْكُ وَلَهُ الْحَمْدُ، لَا إِلَهَ إِلَّا اللَّهُ، وَلَا حَوْلَ وَلَا قُوَّةَ إِلَّا بِاللَّهِ

La ilaha illallah, wallahu akbar, la ilaha illallahu wahdah, la sharika lah, la ilaha illallahu lahulmulku walahulhamd, la ilaha illallah, wala hawla wala quwwata illa billah

'None has the right to be worshipped except Allah and Allah is the greatest None has the right to be worshipped except Allah, alone None has the right to be worshipped except Allah, alone, without partner. None has the right to be worshipped except Allah, to Him belongs all sovereignty and praise None has the right to be worshipped except Allah and there is no might and no power except with Allah'

48. Instruction for the one nearing death

i.e. those around the sick should instruct and encourage him to say the *shahadah*

(145)
'He whose last words are:

لا إلَهَ إلاَّ الله

La ilaha illallah

'None has the right to be worshipped except Allah'
…will enter Paradise'

49. Supplication for one afflicted by a calamity

(146)
إنَّا لله وَإنَّا إلَيْهِ رَاجِعُوْنَ، اللَّهُمَّ أُجُرْنِي فِي مُصِيْبَتِي، وَاخْلُفْ لِي خَيْراً مِنْهَا

Inna lillahi wa inna ilayhi raji'un, allahumma'jurni fi musibati wakhluf li khayran minha

'To Allah we belong and unto Him is our returnO Allah, recompense me for my affliction and replace it for me with something better'

50. When closing the eyes of the deceased

(147)

اللَّهُمَّ اغْفِرْ لِـ فُلان بِاسْمِهِ- وَارْفَعْ دَرَجَتَهُ فِي المَهْدِيِّيْنَ، وَاخْلُفْهُ فِي عَقِبِهِ فِي الغَابِرِيْنَ، وَاغْفِرْ لَنَا وَلَهُ يَا رَبَّ العَالَمِيْنَ، وَافْسَحْ لَهُ فِي قَبْرِهِ وَنَوِّرْ لَهُ فِيهِ

Allahummaghfir li - name the dead - warf'a darajatahu filmahdiyyen, wakhlufhu fi 'aqibihi filghabirin, waghfir lana walahu ya rabbal 'alameen wafsah lahu fi qabrih, wanawwir lahu fih

'O Allah, forgive *here the name of the deceased is mentioned* and raise his rank among the rightly guided, and be a successor to whom he has left behind, and forgive us and him. O Lord of the worlds Make spacious his grave and illuminate it for him'

A successor: one who succeeds another due to the latter's absence or death This is the correct meaning of the word *khalifah*; thus, it is incorrect to believe that Adam is the khalefah (*vicegerent*, as is commonly translated) of Allah on earth because Allah is never absent, and will never die This supplication proves the correct understanding of this term and shows that Allah succeeds us and guards whom we leave behind when we die or are absent

(also refer to supplication #198)

51. Supplication for the deceased at the funeral prayer

(148)

اللَّهُمَّ اغْفِرْ لَهُ وَارْحَمْهُ، وَعَافِهِ وَاعْفُ عَنْهُ، وَأَكْرِمْ نُزُلَهُ، وَوَسِّعْ مُدْخَلَهُ، وَاغْسِلْهُ بِالْمَاءِ وَالثَّلْجِ وَالْبَرَدِ، وَنَقِّهِ مِنَ الْخَطَايَا كَمَا نَقَّيْتَ الثَّوْبَ الْأَبْيَضَ مِنَ الدَّنَسِ، وَأَبْدِلْهُ دَاراً خَيْراً مِنْ دَارِهِ، وَأَهْلاً خَيْراً مِنْ أَهْلِهِ، وَزَوْجاً خَيْراً مِنْ زَوْجِهِ، وَأَدْخِلْهُ الْجَنَّةَ، وَأَعِذْهُ مِنْ عَذَابِ الْقَبْرِ وَعَذَابِ النَّارِ

Allahummaghfir lahu warhamh, wa 'afihi, wa'afu anh, wa akrim nuzulah, wawassi' mudkhalah, waghsilhu bilm'ai waththalji walbarad, wanaqqihi minal khataya kama naqqaytath thawbal abyada minad danas, waabdilhu daran khayran min darih, wa ahlan khayran min ahlih wazawjan khayran min zawjih, waadkhilhul jannah, wa 'aidhhu min adhabil qabr, wadhabin nar

'O Allah, forgive and have mercy upon him, excuse him and pardon him, and make honourable his reception Expand his entry, and cleanse him with water, snow, and ice, and purify him of sin as a white robe is purified of filth Exchange his home for a better home, and his family for a better family, and his spouse for a better spouse Admit him into the Garden, protect him from the punishment of the grave and the torment of the Fire'

(149)

اللّهُمَّ اغْفِرْ لِحَيِّنَا وَمَيِّتِنَا وَشَاهِدِنَا، وَغَائِبِنَا، وَصَغِيرِنَا وَكَبِيرِنَا، وَذَكَرِنَا وَأُنْثَانَا. اللّهُمَّ مَنْ أَحْيَيْتَهُ مِنَّا فَأَحْيِهِ عَلَى الإِسْلامِ، وَمَنْ تَوَفَّيْتَهُ مِنَّا فَتَوَفَّهُ عَلَى الإِيمَانِ، اللّهُمَّ لا تَحْرِمْنَا أَجْرَهُ، وَلا تُضِلَّنَا بَعْدَهُ

Allahummaghfir lihayyina wamayyitina washahidina, waghaibina, wasagherina wakaberina, wa dhakarina wa onthana allahumma man ahyaytahu minna faahyihi 'alal islam, waman tawaffaytahu minna fatawaffahu 'alal iman, allahumma la tahrimna ajrah, wala tudillana b'adah

'O Allah, forgive our living and our dead, those present and those absent, our young and our old, our males and our females. O Allah, whom amongst us You keep alive, then let such a life be upon Islam, and whom amongst us You take unto Yourself, then let such a death be upon faith O Allah, do not deprive us of his reward and do not let us stray after him'

(150)

اللّهُمَّ إِنَّ فُلَانَ بْنَ فُلَانٍ فِي ذِمَّتِكَ، وَحَبْلِ جِوَارِكَ، فَقِهِ مِنْ فِتْنَةِ القَبْرِ وَعَذَابِ النَّارِ، وَأَنْتَ أَهْلُ الوَفَاءِ وَالحَقِّ، فَاغْفِرْ لَهُ وَارْحَمْهُ، إِنَّكَ أَنْتَ الغَفُورُ الرَّحِيمُ

Allahumma inna name the dead fi dhimmatik, wahabli jiwarik, faqihi min fitnatilqabr wa 'adhabinnar, waanta ahlulwafa', walhaq, faghfir lahu warhamh, innaka antal ghaforurrahem

'O Allah, soandso is under Your care and protection so protect him from the trial of the grave and torment of the Fire Indeed You are faithful and truthful Forgive and have mercy upon him, surely You are The Oft Forgiving,, The Most Merciful'

(151)

اللّهُمَّ عَبْدُكَ وَابْنُ أَمَتِكَ، احْتَاجَ إِلَى رَحْمَتِكَ، وَأَنْتَ غَنِيٌّ عَنْ عَذَابِهِ، إِنْ كَانَ مُحْسِنًا فَزِدْ فِي حَسَنَاتِهِ، وَإِنْ كَانَ مُسِيئًا فَتَجَاوَزْ عَنْهُ

Allahumma 'abduka wabnu amatik, ihtaja ila rahmatik, waanta ghaniyyun an adhabih, in kana muhsinan fazid fi hasanatih, wain kana musean fatajawaz anh

'O Allah, Your servant and the son of Your maidservant is in need of Your mercy and You are without need of his punishment If he was righteous then increase his reward and if he was wicked then look over his sins'

52. Supplication for the advancement of reward during the funeral prayer

This supplication is made when the deceased is a baby/child (i.e. one not having reached the age of puberty)

(152)

After seeking forgiveness for the deceased, one can say:

اللّهُمَّ اجْعَلْهُ فَرَطاً وَذُخْراً لِوَالِدَيْهِ، وَشَفِيْعاً مُجَاباً، اللّهُمَّ ثَقِّلْ بِهِ مَوَازِيْنَهُمَا، وَأَعْظِمْ بِهِ أُجُوْرَهُمَا، وَأَلْحِقْهُ بِصَالِحِ المُؤْمِنِيْنَ، وَاجْعَلْهُ فِي كَفَالَةِ إِبْرَاهِيْمَ، وَقِهِ بِرَحْمَتِكَ عَذَابَ الجَحِيْمِ

Allahummaj'alhu faratan, wadhukhran liwalidayh, washafe'an mujaban allahumma thaqqil bihi mawazenahuma wa 'adhim bihi ojorahuma, waalhiqhu bisalihilmu'minen, waj'alhu fee kafalati Ibrahem, waqihi birahmatika adhabal jaheem

'O Allah, make him a preceding reward and a stored treasure for his parents, and an answered intercessor O Allah, through him, make heavy their scales and magnify their reward Unite him with the righteous believers, place him under the care of Ibrahem, and protect him by Your mercy from the torment of Hell'

(153)

al-Hasan used to recite the opening chapter of the Quran (i.e. al-Fatihah) over the child and then supplicates:

اللّهُمَّ اجْعَلْهُ لَنَا فَرَطاً، وَسَلَفاً وَأَجْراً

Allahummaj'alhu lana farata, wasalafan wa ajra

'O Allah, make him a preceding reward, a prepayment and a recompense for us'

53. Condolence

(154)

إنَّ للهِ مَا أَخَذَ، وَلَهُ مَا أَعْطَى، وَكُلُّ شَيْءٍ عِنْدَهُ بِأَجَلٍ مُسَمَّى... فَلْتَصْبِرْ وَلْتَحْتَسِبْ.

Inna lillahi ma akhadh, walahu ma a'ta, wakullu shay'in indahu bi ajalin musamma…faltasbir waltahtasib

'Verily to Allah, belongs what He took and to Him belongs what He gave, and everything with Him has an appointed time……and then he ﷺ ordered for her to be patient and hope for Allah's reward'

The words (*faltasbir waltahtasib*) are commands in the feminine 3rd person form, so they will need to be changed in respect to whom is being addressed

and one can also say:

أَعْظَمَ اللَّهُ أَجْرَكَ، وَأَحْسَنَ عَزَاءَكَ، وَغَفَرَ لِمَيِّتِكَ

'adhamallahu ajrak, waahsana 'aza'k, waghafara limayyitik

'May Allah magnify your reward, make better
your solace and forgive your deceased'
This is the saying of some of the scholars,
not a hadith

54. Placing the deceased in the grave

(155)

بِسْمِ اللَّهِ وَعَلَى سُنَّةِ رَسُولِ اللَّه

Bismillahi wa 'ala sunnati rasulillah

'In the name of Allah and upon the sunnah of
the Messenger of Allah'

55. After burying the deceased

(156)

'After the Prophet ﷺ would bury the deceased
he would stand by the grave and say: 'Seek
forgiveness for your brother and pray that he
remains firm, for he is now being questioned"

56. Visiting the graves

(157)

السَّلامُ عَلَيْكُمْ أَهْلَ الدِّيَارِ مِنَ المُؤْمِنِينَ وَالمُسْلِمِينَ، وَإِنَّا إِنْ شَاءَ
اللَّهُ بِكُمْ لاحِقُونَ، نَسْأَلُ اللَّهَ لَنَا وَلَكُمُ الْعَافِيَةَ

Assalamu 'alaykum ahladdiyari minalmu'minena wal

*muslimeen, wa inna in sha' allahu bikum lahiqon,
nasalullaha lana walakumul 'afiyah*

'Peace be upon you all, O inhabitants of the
graves, amongst the believers and the Muslims.
Verily we will, Allah willing, be united with you,
we ask Allah for wellbeing for us and you'

57. Prayer said during a wind storm

(158)

اللَّهُمَّ إِنِّي أَسْأَلُكَ خَيْرَهَا، وَأَعُوذُ بِكَ مِنْ شَرِّهَا

*Allahumma inni as'aluka khayraha wa a'udhu bika
min sharriha*

'O Allah, I ask You for it's goodness and I take
refuge with You from it's evil'

(159)

اللَّهُمَّ إِنِّي أَسْأَلُكَ خَيْرَهَا، وَخَيْرَ مَا فِيهَا، وَخَيْرَ مَا أُرْسِلَتْ بِهِ، وَأَعُوذُ
بِكَ مِنْ شَرِّهَا، وَشَرِّ مَا فِيهَا، وَشَرِّ مَا أُرْسِلَتْ بِهِ

*Allahumma inni as'aluka khayraha wakhayra ma fiha,
wakhayra ma ursilat bih, wa a'udhu bika min sharriha,
washarri ma fiha washarri ma ursilat bih*

'O Allah, I ask You for it's goodness, the good
within it, and the good it was sent with, and I
take refuge with You from it's evil, the evil within
it, and from the evil it was sent with'

58. Supplication upon hearing thunder

(160)

When Abdullah Ibn Az-Zubayr ؓ used to hear thunder he would stop talking and say:

سُبْحانَ الَّذِي يُسَبِّحُ الرَّعْدُ بِحَمْدِهِ، وَالمَلَائِكَةُ مِنْ خِيفَتِهِ

*Subhanalladhi yusabbihur ra'du bihamdih,
wal mala'ikatu min khifatih*

'How perfect He is, (The One) Whom the thunder declares His perfection with His praise, as do the angles out of fear of Him'

59. Supplication for rain

(161)

اللَّهُمَّ اسْقِنَا غَيْثاً مُغِيْثاً مَرِيْئاً مُرِيْعاً
نَافِعاً غَيْرَ ضَارٍّ، عَاجِلاً غَيْرَ آجِلٍ.

*Allahummasqina ghaythan mughethan mare'an mure'an,
nafian, ghayra dar, 'ajilan ghayra ajil*

'O Allah, send upon us helpful, wholesome and healthy rain, beneficial not harmful rain, now, not later'

(162)

اللَّهُمَّ أَغِثْنَا، اللَّهُمَّ أَغِثْنَا، اللَّهُمَّ أَغِثْنَا

*Allahumma aghithna, allahumma aghithna,
allahumma aghithna*

'O Allah, relieve us, O Allah, relieve us, O Allah, relieve us'

(163)

اللَّهُمَّ اسْقِ عِبَادَكَ وَبَهَائِمَكَ، وَانْشُرْ رَحْمَتَكَ وَأَحْيِي بَلَدَكَ الْمَيِّتَ

Allahummasqi 'ibadak, wabaha'imak, wanshur rahmatak, wa ahyi baladakal mayyit

'O Allah, provide water for Your servants and Your cattle, spread out Your mercy and resurrect Your dead land'

60. Supplication said when it rains

(164)

اللَّهُمَّ صَيِّباً نَافِعاً.

Allahumma sayyiban nafi'a

'O Allah, may it be a beneficial rain cloud'

61. After rainfall

(165)

مُطِرْنَا بِفَضْلِ اللَّهِ وَرَحْمَتِهِ

Mutirna bifadlillahi warahmatih

'We have been given rain by the grace and mercy of Allah'

62. Asking for clear skies

(166)

اللَّهُمَّ حَوَالَيْنَا وَلا عَلَيْنَا، اللَّهُمَّ عَلَى الآكَامِ وَالظِّرَابِ، وَبُطُونِ الأَوْدِيَةِ، وَمَنابِتِ الشَّجَرِ

Allahumma hawalayna wala 'alayna, allahumma 'alalakami wadhdhara'ib, wabutun ilawdiyah, wamanabit ishshajar

'O Allah, let the rain fall around us and not upon us, O Allah, (let it fall) on the pastures, hills, valleys and the roots of trees'

63. Upon sighting the crescent moon

(167)

اللهُ أَكْبَرُ، اللَّهُمَّ أَهِلَّهُ عَلَيْنَا بِالأَمْنِ وَالإِيمَانِ، وَالسَّلامَةِ وَالإِسْلامِ، وَالتَّوْفِيْقِ لِمَا تُحِبُّ وَتَرْضَى، رَبُّنَا وَرَبُّكَ اللهُ

Allahu akbar, allahumma ahillahu 'alayna bilamni waleman, wassalamati walislam, wattawfeiqi lima tuhibbu watarda, rabbuna warabbukallah

'Allah is the greatest O Allah, let the crescent loom above us in safety, faith, peace, and Islam, and in agreement with all that You love and pleases. You Our Lord and your Lord is Allah'

64. Upon breaking fast

(168)

ذَهَبَ الظَّمَأُ، وَابْتَلَّتِ العُرُوقُ، وَثَبَتَ الأَجْرُ إِنْ شَاءَ ٱللَّهُ

Dhahabadhama'o wabtallatil a'uroq, wathabatal ajru in sha' allah

'The thirst has gone and the veins are quenched, and reward is confirmed, if Allah wills'

(169)

'abdullah Ibn amr Ibn Alas 🙏 related that the Messenger of Allah 🙏 said: 'Indeed the fasting person has at the time of breaking fast, a supplication which is not rejected' Ibn Abi Mulaykah 🙏 said: 'I Heard Abdullah Ibn Umar say when he broke his fast:

للَّهُمَّ إِنِّي أَسْأَلُكَ بِرَحْمَتِكَ الَّتِي وَسِعَتْ كُلَّ شَيْءٍ، أَنْ تَغْفِرَ لِي

Allahumma inni as'aluka birahmati kallati wasiat kulla shay', an taghfira li

'O Allah, ask You by Your mercy which envelopes all things, that You forgive me'

65. Supplication before eating

(170)

'When you are about to eat, you should say:

بِسْمِ اللَّهِ

Bismillah

……and if you forget to say it before starting,
then you should say (when you remember):

بِسْـمِ اللَّهِ فِي أَوَّلِهِ وَآخِرِهِ

Bismillahi fi awwalihi wa akhirih

'In the name of Allah in it's beginning and end'

(171)

'Whomever Allah feeds, should say:

اللَّهُـمَّ بَـارِكْ لَنَا فِيهِ وَأَطْعِمْنَا خَيْراً مِنْهُ

*Allahumma barik lana fihi
waataimna khayran minh*

'O Allah, bless it for us and feed us better than it'

…and whomever Allah gives milk to drink
should say:

اللَّهُـمَّ بَارِكْ لَنَا فِيهِ وَزِدْنَا مِنْهُ

Allahumma barik lana fihi wazidna minh

'O Allah, bless it for usand give us more of it'

66. Upon completing the meal

(172)

الحَمْدُ لله الَّذِي أَطْعَمَني هَذَا وَرَزَقَنِيهِ مِنْ غَيْرِ حَوْلٍ مِنِّي وَلَا قُوَّةٍ.

*Alhamdu lillahilladhi atamani hadha warazaqanihi
min ghayri hawlin minni wala quwwah*

'All praise is for Allah who fed me this and
provided it for me without any might nor power

from myself'

(173)

الْحَمْدُ لِلـهِ حَمْداً كَثِيْراً طَيِّباً مُبَارَكاً فِيْهِ، غَيْرَ مَكْفِيٍّ وَلَا مُوَدَّعٍ وَلَا مُسْتَغْنًى عَنْهُ رَبَّنَا

Alhamdu lillahi hamdan katheran tayyiban mubarakan fih, ghayra makfiyyin wala muwaddain, wala mustaghnan anhu rabbuna

'Allah be praised with an abundant beautiful blessed praise, a neverending praise, a praise which we will never bid farewell to and an indispensable praise, He is our Lord'

There are other views as regards to the understanding of this supplication, from them:

Allah be praised with an abundant beautiful blessed praise. He is The One Who is sufficient, feeds and is not fed. The One Who is longed for, along with that which is with Him and The One Who is needed, He is our Lord'

67. Supplication of the guest for the host

(174)

اللَّهُمَّ بَارِكْ لَهُمْ فِيْمَا رَزَقْتَهُمْ، وَاغْفِرْ لَهُمْ وَارْحَمْهُمْ.

Allahumma barik lahum fema razaqtahum, waghfir lahum warhamhum

'O Allah, bless for them, that which You have

provided them, forgive them and have mercy upon them'

68. Supplication said to one offering a drink or to one who intended to do that

(175)

اللّهُمَّ أَطْعِمْ مَنْ أَطْعَمَنِي، وَاسْقِ مَنْ سَقَانِي

Allahumma atAim man atamani wasqi man saqani

'O Allah, feed him who fed me, and provide with drink him who provided me with drink'

69. Supplication said when breaking fast in someone's home

(176)

أَفْطَرَ عِنْدَكُمُ الصَّائِمُونَ وَأَكَلَ طَعَامَكُمُ الْأَبْرَارُ، وَصَلَّتْ عَلَيْكُمُ الْمَلَائِكَةُ

Aftara Indakumus sa'imun, wa akala ta amakumul abrar, wa sallat 'alaykumul malaikah

'May the fasting break their fast in your home, and may the dutiful and pious eat your food, and may the angles send prayers upon you'

70. Supplication said by one fasting when presented with food and does not break his fast

(177)

'If you are not invited (to a meal) then answer If you happen to be fasting, then supplicate (for those present) and if you are not fasting, then eat'

71. Supplication said upon seeing the early or premature fruit

(178)

اللَّهُمَّ بَارِكْ لَنَا فِي ثَمَرِنَا، وَبَارِكْ لَنَا فِي مَدِينَتِنَا، وَبَارِكْ لَنَا فِي صَاعِنَا، وَبَارِكْ لَنَا فِي مُدِّنَا

Allahumma barik lana fi thamarina, wabarik lana fi madina tina, wabarik lana fi saa'ina wabarik lana fi muddina

'O Allah, bless our fruit for us, bless our town for us, bless our *saa* for us and bless our *mudd* for us'
A *saa* is equivalent to four *mudds* and a *mudd* is equivalent to a dry measure of an average man's two palms

72. Supplication said upon sneezing

(179)

'When one of you sneezes he should say:

الحَمْدُ لِله
Alhamdu lillah
'All praise if for Allah'
……and his brother or companion should say to him:
يَرْحَمُكَ اللَّهُ
Yarhamukallah
'May Allah have mercy upon you'
……and he (i.e. the one who sneezed) replies back to him:
يَهْدِيكُمُ اللَّهُ وَيُصْلِحُ بَالكُمْ
Yahdikumullahu wa yuslihu balakum
'May Allah guide you and rectify your condition'

73. Supplication said to the newlywed

(180)
بَارَكَ اللَّهُ لَكَ، وَبَارَكَ عَلَيْكَ، وَجَمَعَ بَيْنَكُمَا فِي خَيْرٍ
Barakallahu lak, wabaraka 'alayk, wajama baynakuma fi khayr
'May Allah bless for you (your spouse) and bless you, and may He unite both of you in goodness'

74. The groom's supplication on the wedding night or when buying an animal

(181)

When you marry a woman or buy a maidservant, you should say:

اللَّهُمَّ إِنِّي أَسْأَلُكَ خَيْرَهَا، وَخَيْرَ مَا جَبَلْتَهَا عَلَيْهِ، وَأَعُوذُ بِكَ مِنْ شَرِّهَا، وَشَرِّ مَا جَبَلْتَهَا عَلَيْهِ

Allahumma inni as'aluka khayraha wakhayra ma jabaltaha 'alayh, wa a'udhu bika min sharriha washarri ma jabaltaha 'alayh

'O Allah, I ask You for the goodness within her and the goodness that you have made her inclined towards, and I take refuge with You from the evil within her and the evil that you have made her inclined towards'

...and if you buy a camel, then you should take hold of it's hump and say likewise'

75. Supplication before sexual intercourse

(182)

بِسْمِ اللهِ اللَّهُمَّ جَنِّبْنَا الشَّيْطَانَ، وَجَنِّبِ الشَّيْطَانَ مَا رَزَقْتَنَا

Bismillah, allahumma jannibnash shaytan, wajannibishshaytana ma razaqtana

'In the name of Allah O Allah, keep the devil away from us and keep the devil away from what you have blessed us with'

76. When angry

(183)

أَعُوذُ بِاللهِ مِنَ الشَّيْطَانِ الرَّجِيمِ

A'udhu billahi minash shaytanir rajeem

'I take refuge with Allah from the accursed devil'

77. Supplication said upon seeing someone in trial or tribulation

This supplication is to be said to one's self, not directly to the one in trial or tribulation

(184)

الحَمْدُ للهِ الَّذِي عَافَانِي مِمَّا ابْتَلاكَ بِهِ، وَفَضَّلَنِي عَلَى كَثِيرٍ مِمَّنْ خَلَقَ تَفْضِيلاً

Alhamdu lillahilladhi afani mimmabtalaka bih, wafaddalani 'ala kathirin mimman khalaqa tafdila

'All praise is for Allah Who saved me from that which He tested you with and Who most certainly favoured me over much of His creation'

78. Remembrance said at a sitting or gathering…etc

(185)

Ibn Aumar ؓ said: It would be counted that the Messenger of Allah ﷺ would say one hundred times at any one sitting before getting up:

رَبِّ اغْفِرْ لِي وَتُبْ عَلَيَّ، إِنَّكَ أَنْتَ التَّوَّابُ الغَفُورُ.

Rabbighfir li watub 'alay, innaka antattawwa bulghafur

'O my Lord, forgive me and turn towards me (to accept my repentance) Verily You are The Oft Returning The Oft Forgiving'

79. Supplication for the expiation of sins said at the conclusion of a sitting or gathering…etc

(186)

سُبْحَانَكَ اللَّهُمَّ وَبِحَمْدِكَ، أَشْهَدُ أَنْ لا إِلَهَ إِلاَّ أَنْتَ أَسْتَغْفِرُكَ وَأَتُوبُ إِلَيْكَ

Subhanakallahumma wabihamdik, ashhadu an la ilaha illa ant, astaghfiruka wa atubu ilayk

'How perfect You are O Allah, and I praise You I bear witness that None has the right to be worshipped except You I seek Your forgiveness and turn to You in repentance'

Cont. 79. Supplication for concluding all sittings

(187)

Aishah said: Whenever The Messenger of Allah would betake a seat, read Quran or pray, he would always conclude it with certain words, I (i.e. Aishah) said: O Messenger of Allah, I have noticed that whenever you betake a seat, read Quran or pray, you always conclude it with these words He said: Yes, whoever speaks good, it (i.e. the supplication) will be a seal for that goodness and whoever speaks ill, it will be an atonement for him'

سُبْحَانَكَ وَبِحَمْدِكَ، لا إِلَهَ إِلاَّ أَنْتَ أَسْتَغْفِرُكَ وَأَتُوبُ إِلَيْكَ

Subhanaka wabihamdik, la ilaha illa anta astaghfiruka wa atubu ilayk

'How perfect You are and I praise You None has the right to be worshipped except You, I seek Your forgiveness and turn in repentance to You'

80. Returning a supplication of forgiveness

(188)

'Abdullah Ibn Sarjis said: 'I went to see the Prophet and ate from his food and then said to him:

غَفَرَ اللَّهُ لَكَ يَا رَسُولَ اللَّهِ

Ghafarallahu laka ya rasulallah

'May Allah forgive you, O Messenger of Allah'

......he ﷺ replied:

وَلَكَ

walak

'and you'

81. Supplication said to one who does you a favour

(189)

'If someone does you a favour and you say:

جَزَاكَ اللَّهُ خَيْرًا.

Jazakallahu khayran

'May Allah reward you with goodness'

......then you have indeed excelled in praising him'

82. Protection from the Dajjal

Dajjal: among the great signs of the last hour and the greatest trials to befall mankind, which every Prophet has warned about. Most of mankind will follow him. He will appear from Asbahan, Iran at the time when Muslims will conquer Constantinople. He will be given special powers and will make the truth seem false and vice versa. He will claim to be righteous and then he will claim prophethood and finally, divinity. From his features is that he will be blind in his right eye which is a definite proof that contradicts his claim to be Allah as it is a sign of imperfection. The word Kafir will be written between his eyes which every believer, literate or illiterate will recognise.

(190)

'Whoever memorises the first ten verses of surat al-Kahf will be protected from Dajjal'
One should also seek refuge with Allah from the tribulations of the Dajjal after the last tashahhud in prayer (Refer to supplications #55 & #56)

83. Supplication said to one who pronounces his love for you, for Allah's sake

(191)

أَحَبَّكَ الَّذِي أَحْبَبْتَنِي لَهُ

Ahabbakalladhi ahbabtani lah

'May He, for whom you have loved me, love you'

84. Supplication said to one who has offered you some of his wealth

(192)

بَارَكَ اللّٰهُ لَكَ فِي أَهْلِكَ وَمَالِكَ

Barakallahu laka fi ahlika wamalik

'May Allah bless for you, your family and wealth'

85. Supplication said to the debtor when his debt is settled

(193)

بَارَكَ اللّٰهُ لَكَ فِي أَهْلِكَ وَمَالِكَ، إِنَّمَا جَـزَاءُ السَّلَفِ الحَمْدُ والأَداء

Barakallahu laka fi ahlika wamalik, innama jaza'us salafilhamdu walada'

'May Allah bless for you, your family and wealth Surely commendation and payment are the reward for a loan'

86. Supplication for fear of shirk

shirk: to associate others with Allah in those things which are specific to Him This can occur in (1) belief, eg to believe that other than Allah has the power to benefit or harm, (2) speech, eg to swear by other than Allah and (3) action, eg to bow or prostrate to other than Allah

(194)

اللَّهُمَّ إِنِّي أَعوذُبِكَ أَنْ أُشْرِكَ بِكَ وَأَنا أَعْلَمُ، وَأَسْتَغْفِرُكَ لِما لا أَعْلَمُ

*Allahumma inni a'udhu bika an ushrika bika wa anna
'alam, wa astaghfiruka lima la 'alam*

'O Allah, I take refuge in You lest I should
commit *shirk* with You knowingly and I seek
Your forgiveness for what I do unknowingly'

87. Returning a supplication after having bestowed a gift or charity upon someone

(195)

Aishah ؓ reported that the Messenger of Allah
ﷺ was given a sheep and he ordered for it's
distribution When the servant would come back
(from distributing it), Aishah would ask: *'What
did they say?'*, he replied: *They would supplicate:*

بارَكَ الله فيكم

Barakallahu fikum

'May Allah bless you all'

...*Aishah would then say:*

وفيهم بارَكَ الله

Wafihim barakallah

'and may Allah bless them'

...*we return their supplication in a similar way
and our reward remains with us*

88. Forbiddance of ascribing things to omens

This supplication is used whenever one initially thinks a casual event or occurrence to foretell good or evil, using it as a basis to determine which action he should undertake, but he then denounces such a link, relies on Allah and then says this supplication as an expiation for this act, since it falls under the category of *shirk*

(196)

اللَّهُمَّ لا طَيْرَ إلاَّ طَيْرُك، وَلا خَيْرَ إلاَّ خَيْرُك، وَلا إلهَ غَيْرُك

Allahumma la tayra illa tayruk, wala khayra illa khayruk, wala ilaha ghayruk

'O Allah, there is no omen but there is reliance on You, there is no good except Your good and none has the right to be worshipped except You'

89. Supplication said when mounting an animal or any means of transport

(197)

بِسْمِ اللهِ وَالْحَمْدُ لله، سُبْحانَ الَّذي سَخَّرَ لَنا هذا وَما كُنَّا لَهُ مُقْرِنين، وَإِنَّا إلى رَبِّنا لَمُنْقَلِبون، الحَمْدُ لله، الحَمْدُ لله، الحَمْدُ لله، اللَّهُ أَكْبَر، اللَّهُ أَكْبَر، اللَّهُ أَكْبَر، سُبْحانَكَ اللَّهُمَّ إِنِّي ظَلَمْتُ نَفْسي فَاغْفِرْ لي، فَإِنَّهُ لا يَغْفِرُ الذُّنوبَ إلاَّ أَنْت

Bismillah, walhamdu lillah, subhanalladhi sakhkhara

lana hadha wama kunna lahu muqrinen, wainna ila rabbina lamunqalibon, alhamdu lillah, alhamdu lillah, alhamdu lillah, allahu akbar, allahu akbar, allahu akbar, subhanakallahumma inni dhalamtu nafsi faghfir li fainnahu la yaghfiruthdhunoba illa ant

'In the name of Allah and all praise is for Allah. How perfect He is, the One Who has placed this (transport) at our service and we ourselves would not have been capable of that, and to our Lord is our final destiny. All praise is for Allah, All praise is for Allah, All praise is for Allah, Allah is the greatest, Allah is the greatest, Allah is the greatest. How perfect You are, O Allah, verily I have wronged my soul, so forgive me, for surely none can forgive sins except You'

90. Supplication for travel

(198)

اللَّهُ أَكْبَرُ، اللَّهُ أَكْبَرُ، اللَّهُ أَكْبَرُ سُبْحَانَ الَّذِي سَخَّرَ لَنَا هَذَا وَمَا كُنَّا لَهُ مُقْرِنِينَ وَإِنَّا إِلَى رَبِّنَا لَمُنْقَلِبُونَ، اللَّهُمَّ إِنَّا نَسْأَلُكَ فِي سَفَرِنَا هَذَا الْبِرَّ وَالتَّقْوَى، وَمِنَ الْعَمَلِ مَا تَرْضَى، اللَّهُمَّ هَوِّنْ عَلَيْنَا سَفَرَنَا هَذَا وَاطْوِ عَنَّا بُعْدَهُ، اللَّهُمَّ أَنْتَ الصَّاحِبُ فِي السَّفَرِ، وَالْخَلِيفَةُ فِي الْأَهْلِ، اللَّهُمَّ إِنِّي أَعُوذُ بِكَ مِنْ وَعْثَاءِ السَّفَرِ، وَكَآبَةِ الْمَنْظَرِ، وَسُوءِ الْمُنْقَلَبِ فِي الْمَالِ وَالْأَهْلِ

Allahu akbar, Allahu akbar, Allahu akbar, subhanalladhi sakhkhara lana hadha wama kunna

*lahu muqrinen, wa inna ila rabbina lamun qalibun,
allahumma inna nas'aluka fi safarina hadha albirra
wattaqwa, waminal amali ma tarda, allahumma
hawwin 'alayna safarana hadha, watwi anna budah,
allahumma antassahibu fissafar, walkhalifatu filahl,
allahumma inni a'udhu bika min wathaissafar,
wakaabatil mandhar, wasoo'il munqalabi filmali wal ahl*

'Allah is the greatest, Allah is the greatest, Allah is the greatest, How perfect He is, The One Who has placed this (transport) at our service, and we ourselves would not have been capable of that, and to our Lord is our final destiny O Allah, we ask You for *birr* and *taqwa* in this journey of ours, and we ask You for deeds which please You O Allah, facilitate our journey and let us cover it's distance quickly O Allah, You are The Companion on the journey and The Successor over the family, O Allah, I take refuge with You from the difficulties of travel, from having a change of hearts and being in a bad predicament, and I take refuge in You from an ill fated outcome with wealth and family'

birr and taqwa: two comprehensive terms which individually, refer to all good actions and obedience i.e. performing the commanded actions and avoiding the prohibited actions When combined together, *birr* refers to doing those actions which have been commanded and *taqwa* refers to avoiding those actions which have been prohibited

A successor: one who succeeds another due to the latter's absence or death This is the correct meaning of the word *khalifah*; thus, it is incorrect to believe that Adam is the khalifah (*vicegerent*, as is commonly translated) of Allah on earth because Allah is never absent, and will never die This supplication proves the correct understanding of this term and shows that Allah succeeds us and guards whom we leave behind when we die or are absent

…upon returning the same supplication is recited with the following addition:

آيِبُونَ تَائِبُونَ عَابِدُونَ لِرَبِّنَا حَامِدُونَ

Ayibuna, taibuna, abiduna, lirabbina hamidun

'We return, repent, worship and praise our Lord'

91. Supplication upon entering a town or village…etc

(199)

اللّـهُمَّ رَبَّ السَّمـواتِ السَّبْـعِ وَما أَظْلَلَـن، وَرَبَّ الأَراضيـنَ السَّبْـعِ وَما أَقْلَلـن، وَرَبَّ الشَّيـاطينِ وَما أَضْلَلـن، وَرَبَّ الرِّياحِ وَما ذَرَيْـن، أَسْأَلُـكَ خَيْـرَ هذهِ الْقَرْيَةِ وَخَيْـرَ أَهْلِـها، وَخَيْـرَ ما فيها، وَأَعـوذُ

بِكَ مِنْ شَرِّها وَشَرِّ أَهْلِها، وَشَرِّ ما فيها

Allahumma rabbassamawatis saba'i wama adhlaln, warabbal aradinas saba'i wama aqlalna, warabbash shayatini wama adlalna, warabbarriyahi wama dharayn, as'aluka khayra hadhihilqaryah, wakhayra ahlilha wakhayra ma fiha, wa a'udhu bika min sharriha washarri ahliha, washarri ma fiha

'O Allah, Lord of the seven heavens and all that they envelop, Lord of the seven earths and all that they carry, Lord of the devils and all whom they misguide, Lord of the winds and all whom they whisk away I ask You for the goodness of this village, the goodness of its inhabitants and for all the goodness found within it and I take refuge with You from the evil of this village, the evil of its inhabitants and from all the evil found within it'

92. When entering the market

(200)

لا إلهَ إلاّ اللهُ وحدَهُ لا شريكَ لهُ، لهُ المُلْكُ ولهُ الحَمْدُ، يُحْيِي وَيُمِيتُ وَهُوَ حَيٌّ لا يَمُوتُ، بِيَدِهِ الخَيْرُ وَهُوَ على كلِّ شيءٍ قدير

La ilaha illallah, wahdahu la sharika lah, lahul mulku walahul hamd, yuhyi wayumitu wahuwa hayyun la yamut, biyadihil khayru wahuwa 'ala kulli shay'in qadir

'None has the right to be worshipped except Allah, alone, without partner, to Him belongs

all sovereignty and praise He gives life and
causes death, and He is living and does not
die In His hand is all good and He is over all
things, omnipotent'

93. Supplication for when the mounted animal (or mean of transport) stumbles

(201)

بِسْمِ اللهِ

Bismillah

'In the name of Allah'

94. Supplication of the traveller for the resident

(202)

أَسْتَوْدِعُكُمُ اللهَ الَّذي لا تَضيعُ وَدائِعُه

Astawdiukumullah, alladhi la tadee'u wada'i 'uh

'I place you in the trust of Allah, whose trust is never misplaced'

95. Supplication of the resident for the traveller

(203)

أَسْتَـوْدِعُ اللهَ ديـنَكَ وَأمانَتَكَ، وَخَـواتيمَ عَمَلِك

Astawdi'ullaha dinak, waamanatak, wakhawatema amalik

'I place your religion, your faithfulness and the ends of your deeds in the trust of Allah'

(204)

زَوَّدَكَ اللهُ التَّقْوَى، وَغَفَرَ ذَنْبَكَ، وَيَسَّرَ لَكَ الـخَيْرَ حَيْثُمَا كُنْتَ

Zawwadakallahut taqwa, waghafara thanbak, wayassara lakalkhayra haythuma kunt

'May Allah endow you with *taqwa*, forgive your sins and facilitate all good for you, wherever you be'

taqwa: a comprehensive term which refers to all good actions and obedience i.e. performing the commanded actions and avoiding the prohibited actions

96. Remembrance while ascending or descending

(205)

Jabir ؓ said: While ascending, we would say:

اللهُ أَكْبَر

Allahu akbar

'Allah is the greatest'

…and when descending, we would say:

سُبْحانَ الله

Subhanallah

'How perfect Allah is'

97. Prayer of the traveller as dawn approaches

(206)

سَمِعَ سَامِعٌ بِحَمْدِ اللهِ وَحُسْنِ بَلائِهِ عَلَيْنا، رَبَّنا صَاحِبْنا وَأَفْضِل عَلَيْنا عائِذاً بِاللهِ مِنَ النارِ

Sami'a saami'un bihamdillahi wahusni bala'ihi 'alayna Rabbana sahibna wa'afdil 'alayna a'idhan billahi minannar

'May a witness, be witness to our praise of Allah for His favours and bounties upon us Our Lord, protect us, show favour on us and deliver us from every evil I take refuge in Allah from the fire'

98. Stopping or lodging somewhere

(207)

أَعـوذُ بِكَلِـماتِ اللهِ التَـامَاتِ مِنْ شَرِّ ما خَلَـق

A'udhu bikalimatillahittammati min sharri ma khalaq

'I take refuge in Allah's perfect words from the evil that He has created'

99. While returning from travel

(208)

Ibn Umar ؓ reported that the Messenger of Allah ﷺ on return from a battle or from performing the pilgrimage would say at every high point:

اللَّهُ أَكْبَرُ، اللَّهُ أَكْبَرُ، اللَّهُ أَكْبَرُ

Allahu akbar, Allahu akbar, Allahu akbar

'Allah is the greatest, Allah is the greatest, Allah is the greatest'

...and then he would say:

لا إلَهَ إلا اللَّهُ وَحْـدَهُ لا شَرِيكَ لهُ، لهُ المُلكُ ولهُ الحَمْد، وهوَ على كُلِّ شَيءٍ قَـدير، آيِبـونَ تائِبـونَ عابِدونَ لِرَبِّنا حامِـدون، صَدَقَ اللَّهُ وَعْـدَه، وَنَصَـرَ عَبْـدَه، وَهَزَمَ الأَحْـزابَ وَحْـدَه

La ilaha illallahu wahdahu la sharika lah, lahulmulku walahulhamd, wahuwa 'ala kulli shay'in qadir, a'yibuna taa'ibun, abidun, lirabbina hamidun, sadaqallahu wadah, wanasara abdah, wahazamal ahzaba wahdah

'None has the right to be worshipped except Allah, alone, without partner. To Him belongs all sovereignty and praise, and He is over all things omnipotent. We return, repent, worship and praise our Lord. Allah fulfilled His promise, aided His Servant, and singlehandedly defeated the allies'

100. What to say upon receiving pleasing or displeasing news

(209)

When he ﷺ used to receive pleasant news, he ﷺ would say:

الْحَمْـدُ لِلهِ الَّذِي بِنِـعْمَتِهِ تَتِمُّ الصَّالِحات

Alhamdu lillahilladhi bini'amatihi tatimmus salihat

'All Praise is for Allah by whose favour good works are accomplished'

…and upon receiving displeasing news, he ﷺ would say:

الْحَمْـدُ لِلهِ عَلَى كُلِّ حَال

Alhamdu lillahi 'ala kulli hal

'All Praise is for Allah in all circumstances'

101. Excellence of sending prayers upon the Prophet ﷺ

(210)

The Prophet ﷺ said: 'Whoever sends a prayer upon me, Allah sends ten upon him'

(211)

He ﷺ also said: 'Do not take my grave as a place of habitual ceremony Send prayers upon me, for verily your prayers reach me wherever you are'

He ﷺ also said: 'A miser is one whom when I am mentioned to him, fails to send prayers upon me'

102. Excellence of spreading the Islamic greeting

(213)

The Messenger of Allah ﷺ said: 'You shall not enter paradise until you believe, and you shall not believe until you love one another Shall I not inform you of something, if you were to act upon it, you will indeed achieve mutual love for one another? Spread the greeting amongst yourselves'

(214)

Ammar ؓ said: 'Three characteristics, whoever combines them, has completed his faith: to be just, to spread greetings to all people and to spend (charitably) out of the little you have'

(215)

'Abdullah Ibn Amr ؓ reported that a man asked the Prophet ﷺ: 'Which Islam is the best?' He ﷺ replied: Feed (the poor), and greet those whom you know as well as those whom you do not'

103. Supplication said upon hearing a rooster crow or the braying of an ass

(216)

'If you hear the crow of a rooster, ask Allah for his bounty for it has seen an angel and if you hear the braying of an ass, seek refuge in Allah for it has seen a devil'

104. Supplication upon hearing the barking of dogs at night

(217)

'If you hear the barking of dogs or the braying of asses at night, seek refuge in Allah for they see what you do not'

105. Supplication said for one you have insulted

(218)

اللَّهُمَّ فَأَيُّمَا مُؤْمِنٍ سَبَبْتُهُ فَاجْعَلْ ذَلِكَ لَهُ قُرْبَةً إِلَيكَ يَوْمَ القِيَامةِ

Allahumma fa ayyuma mu'minin sababtuhu faj'al dhalika lahu qurbatan ilayka yawmal qiyamah

'O Allah, to any believer whom I have insulted, let that be cause to draw him near to You on the Day of Resurrection'

106. The etiquette of praising a fellow Muslim

(219)

He ﷺ said: 'If anyone of you is impelled to praise his brother, then he should say: 'I deem soandso to be…and Allah is his reckoner…and I don't praise anyone, putting it (i.e. my praising) forward, in front of Allah's commendation, however I assume him so and so'…if he knows that of him'

107. Supplication said between the Yemeni corner and the black stone (at the Kabah)

(220)

The Prophet ﷺ used to say between the Yemeni corner and the black stone:

﴿رَبَّنَا آتِنَا فِي الدُّنْيَا حَسَنَةً وَفِي الْآخِرَةِ حَسَنَةً وَقِنَا عَذَابَ النَّارِ﴾
(Rabbana atina fi alddunya hasanatan wafi alakhirati hasanatan waqina adhaba alnnar)

[AlBaqarah: 201]

'O our Lord, grant us the best in this life and the best in the next life, and protect us from the punishment of the Fire'

108. Supplication said when at Mount Safa & Mount Marwah

(221)

Jabir ؓ said when describing the Prophet's ﷺ pilgrimage: '…and when he approached mount *Safa* he recited:

﴿إِنَّ الصَّفَا وَالمَرْوَةَ مِنْ شَعَائِرِ اللهِ…﴾

(Innassafa wal marwata min sh'airi Allah …)

أبدأ بما بدأ الله به

Abda' bima badallahu bih

'Indeed Safa and Marwah are from the places of worship of Allah…'

'I begin with what Allah began with'

…so he started with *Safa* and climed it until he could see the Kabah, he then faced it and said:

اللهُ أَكْبَرُ، اللهُ أَكْبَرُ، اللهُ أَكْبَرُ

Allahu akbar, Allahu akbar, Allahu akbar

'Allah is the greatest, Allah is the greatest, Allah is the greatest'

…and then he would say the following three times making a supplication (one should make a personal supplication) after each time:

لَا إِلَهَ إِلَّا اللهُ وَحْدَهُ لَا شَرِيكَ لَهُ، لَهُ المُلْكُ وَلَهُ الحَمْدُ وهُوَ عَلَى كُلِّ شَيْءٍ قَدِيرٌ، لَا إِلَهَ إِلَّا اللهُ وَحْدَهُ أَنْجَزَ وَعْدَهُ، وَنَصَرَ عَبْدَهُ وَهَزَمَ الأَحْزَابَ وَحْدَهُ

La ilaha illallahu wahdahu la sharika lah, lahulmulku

walahulhamd, wahuwa 'ala kulli shay'in qadir, la ilaha illallahu wahdah, anjaza w'adah, wanasara 'abdah, wahazamal ahzaba wahdah

'None has the right to be worshipped except Allah, alone, without partner. To Him belongs all sovereignty and praise and He is over all things omnipotent. None has the right to be worshipped except Allah alone. He fulfilled His promise, aided His Servant and singlehandedly defeated the enemies'

…he ﷺ would repeat this action at *Marwah*

109. The Day of Arafah

(222)

'The best of supplications is the supplication on the day of arafah and the best which I and the Prophets before me have said (is):

لَا إِلَهَ إِلَّا اللَّهُ وَحْدَهُ لَا شَرِيكَ لَهُ، لَهُ الْمُلْكُ وَلَهُ الْحَمْدُ وهُوَ عَلَى كُلِّ شَيْءٍ قَدِيرٌ.

La ilaha illallahu wahdahu la sharika lah, lahulmulku walahulhamd, wahuwa 'ala kulli shay'in qadir

'None has the right to be worshipped except Allah, alone, without partner. To Him belongs all praise and sovereignty and He is over all things omnipotent'

110. At the Sacred Site (al-Mashar al-Haram)

(223)

Jabir said: 'He rode al-Qaswa until he reached AlMashar AlHaram, he then faced the qiblah, supplicated to Allah, and extoled His greatness and oneness He stood until the sun shone but left before it rose'

al-Qaswa: The name of the Prophet's *camel*

111. When throwing each pebble at the Jamarat

i.e. Stoning the three areas at Mina during Hajj

(224)

Every time the Prophet threw a pebble at any of the three jamarat, he would say:

اللهُ أَكْبَر

Allahu akbar

'Allah is the greatest'

…on completion of the first jamarah, he advanced a little, stood facing the qiblah, raised his hands and supplicated He also did this after the second jamarah but not the third'

112. At the black stone

(225)

'The Prophet ﷺ circled the Kabah on a camel, every time he reached the black stone he would point to it with his staff and say:

اللهُ أَكْبَر

Allahu akbar

'Allah is the greatest'

113. Supplication made against an enemy

(226)

اللَّهُمَّ مُنْزِلَ الكِتَابِ سَرِيعَ الحِسَابِ اهْزِمِ الأَحْزَابَ اللَّهُمَّ اهْزِمْهُمْ وَزَلْزِلْهُمْ

Allahumma munzilal kitab, sari'al hisab, ihzimal ahzab, allahummahzimhum wazalzilhum

'O Allah, Revealer of the Book, Swift at reckoning, defeat the confederates O Allah, defeat them and convulse them'

114. What to say when in fear of a people

(227)

اللَّهُمَّ اكْفِنِيهِمْ بِمَا شِئْتَ

Allahummakfinihim bima shi'ta

'O Allah, protect me from them with what

You choose'

115. What to say at times of amazement and delight

(228)

سُبْحَانَ اللّٰهِ!

Subhanallah!

'How perfect Allah is'

(229)

اللّٰهُ أَكْبَرُ!

Allahu akbar

'Allah is the greatest'

116. What to do upon receiving pleasant news

(230)

The Prophet ﷺ would prostrate in gratitude to Allah ﷻ upon receiving news which pleased him or which caused pleasure

117. What to say and do when feeling some pain in the body

(231)

'Place your hand at the site of the pain and say:

بِسْمِ اللَّهِ (ثلاثًا)

Bismillah (three times)

'In the name of Allah' (three times)

...the supplicate seven times:

أَعُوذُ بِاللَّهِ وَقُدْرَتِهِ مِنْ شَرِّ مَا أَجِدُ وَأُحَاذِرُ (سبع مرات)

A'udhu billahi waqudratih min sharri ma ajidu wa uhadhir (seven times)

'I take refuge in Allah and within His omnipotence from the evil that I feel and am wary of' (seven times)

118. What to say when in fear of afflicting something or someone with one's eye

The Evil Eye: To look at something and be impressed with it, causing harm to befall it. This "looking" *may or may not* involve jealousy, and can occur *unintentionally, indeed be part of a person's nature!* A person can even inflict harm *on himself*

From the supplications for the protection against the Evil Eye:

اللَّهُمَّ بَارِكْ عَلَيْهِ

Allahumma barik 'alayh

'O Allah, send blessing upon him'

مَا شَاءَ اللَّهُ، لَا قُوَّةَ إِلَّا بِاللَّهِ

Ma shallah, la quwwata illa billah

'(this is) that which Allah has willed, there is no power except with Allah'

(232)
'If you see something from your brother, yourself or wealth which you find impressing, then invoke blessings for it, for the evil eye is indeed true'

119. Etiquette of retiring for the night

(233)
'When night falls (i.e. al-Maghrib), restrain your children (from going out) because at such time the devils spread about. After a period of time has passed, let them be. Shut your doors and mention Allah's name, for verily the devil does not open a shut door, tie up your waterskins and mention Allah's name, cover your vessels with anything and mention Allah's name and put out your lamps'

120. The Talbiyah

(234)
لَبَّيْكَ اللَّهُمَّ لَبَّيْكَ، لَبَّيْكَ لَا شَرِيكَ لَكَ لَبَّيْكَ، إِنَّ الحَمْدَ وَالنِّعْمَةَ، لَكَ وَالمُلْكَ، لَا شَرِيكَ لَكَ

Labbaykallahumma labbayk, labbayka la sharika laka

labbayk, innalhamda wanni'mata laka walmulk, la sharika lak

'Here I am O Allah, (in response to Your call), here I am Here I am, You have no partner, here I am Verily all praise, grace and sovereignty belong to You. You have no partner'

121. What to say when startled

(235)

لَا إِلَهَ إِلَّا اللَّهُ

La ilaha illallah

'None has the right to be worshipped except Allah'

122. What is said to a disbeliever when he sneezes

(236)

يَهْدِيكُمُ اللَّهُ وَيُصْلِحُ بَالَكُمْ

Yahdekum wayuslihu balakum

'May Allah guide you and rectify your condition'

123. Returning a greeting to a disbeliever

(237)

'When the people of the Book greet you, reply by saying:

وَعَلَيْكُم
Walaykum
'And upon you'

124. When insulted while fasting

(238)

إِنِّي صَائِمٌ، إِنِّي صَائِمٌ
Inni sa'im, inni sa'im
'I am fasting, I am fasting'

125. When slaughtering or offering a sacrifice

(239)

بِسْمِ اللهِ وَاللهُ أَكْبَرُ اللَّهُمَّ مِنْكَ وَلَكَ اللَّهُمَّ تَقَبَّلْ مِنِّي
Bismillah wallahu akbar, allahumma minka walak, allahumma taqabbal minni
'In the name of Allah, and Allah is the greatest O Allah, (it is) from You and belongs to You, O Allah, accept this from me'

126. What is said to ward off the deception of the Obstinate Shaytans

(240)

أَعُوذُ بِكَلِمَاتِ اللهِ التَّامَّاتِ الَّتِي لَا يُجَاوِزُهُنَّ بَرٌّ وَلَا فَاجِرٌ مِنْ شَرِّ مَا خَلَقَ، وَبَرَأَ وَذَرَأَ، وَمِنْ شَرِّ مَا يَنْزِلُ مِنَ السَّمَاءِ وَمِنْ شَرِّ مَا يَعْرُجُ

فِيهَا، ومِنْ شَرِّ مَا ذَرَأَ فِي الأَرْضِ ومِنْ شَرِّ مَا يَخْرُجُ مِنْهَا، ومِنْ شَرِّ فِتَنِ اللَّيْلِ والنَّهارِ، ومِنْ شَرِّ كُلِّ طارِقٍ إلَّا طَارِقاً يَطْرُقُ بِخَيْرٍ يَا رَحْمَنُ

A'udhu bikalimatillahittammat, allate la yujawizuhunna barrun wala fajir min sharri ma khalaq, wabara'a wadhara'a, wamin sharri ma yanzilu minassama', wamin sharri ma yaruju fiha, wamin sharri ma dhara filard, wamin sharri ma yakhruju minha, wamin sharri fitnanillayli wannahar, wamin sharri kulli tariqin illa tariqan yatruqu bikhayrin ya rahman

'I take refuge within Allah's perfect words which no righteous or unrighteous person can transgress, from all the evil that He has created, made and originated (I take refuge) from the evil that descends from the sky and the evil that rises up to it (I take refuge) from the evil that is spread on Earth and the evil that springs from her, and I take refuge from the evil of the tribulations of night and day, and the evil of one who visits at night except the one who brings good, O Merciful One'

127. Seeking forgiveness and repentance

(241)
'The Messenger of Allah ﷺ said: 'By Allah, I seek forgiveness and repent to Allah, more than seventy times a day'

(242)

He ﷺ also said: 'O People, Repent! Verily I repent to Allah, a hundred times a day'

(243)

He ﷺ also said: 'Whoever says:

أَسْتَغْفِرُ اللَّهَ الَّذِي لَا إِلَهَ إِلَّا هُوَ الحَيُّ القَيُّومُ وَأَتُوبُ إِلَيْهِ

Astaghfirullah alladhi la ilaha illa huwalhayyul qayyumu wa atubu ilayh

'I seek Allah's forgiveness, besides whom, none has the right to be worshipped except He, The Ever Living, The Self Subsisting and Supporter of all, and I turn to Him in repentance' …Allah would forgive him even if he was one who fled during the advance of an army'

(244)

He ﷺ said: 'The nearest the Lord comes to His servant is in the middle of the night, so if you are able to be of those who remember Allah at that time, then be so'

(245)

He ﷺ also said: 'The nearest a servant is to his Lord is when he is prostrating, so supplicate much therein'

(246)

He ﷺ also said: 'verily my heart becomes preoccupied, and verily I seek Allah's forgiveness a hundred times a day'

preoccupied: i.e. in a state of *'forgetfulness'*
The Prophet ﷺ always used to increase in his remembrance of his Lord, in attaining a nearness to Allah and having consciousness of Allah to the extent that if this intensity lessened in anyway, he would regard it as a sin and would then race to seek forgiveness from Allah

128. Excellence of remembrance and glorification of Allah

(247)

Abu Hurayrah ؓ reported that the Messenger of Allah ﷺ said: 'Whoever says:

لَا إِلٰهَ إِلَّا اللّٰهُ وَحْدَهُ لَا شَرِيكَ لَـهُ، لَهُ الْمُلْكُ وَلَهُ الْحَمْد، وَهُوَ عَلَى كُلِّ شَيْءٍ قَدِيرٌ. (مائة مرة)

La ilaha illallahu wahdahu la sharika lah, lahulmulku walahulhamd, wahuwa 'ala kulli shay'in qadir

(one hundred times)

'None has the right to be worshipped except Allah, alone, without partner To Him belongs all sovereignty and praise and He is over all

things omnipotent'
…a hundred times during the day, has the reward of freeing ten slaves, a hundred good deeds are recorded for him and a hundred bad deeds are wiped away and he has gained refuge from the devil that day until evening and none shall come with anything better except someone who has done more'

(248)

'Whoever says:

سُبْحَانَ اللهِ وَبِحَمْدِهِ (مائة مرة في اليوم)

Subhanallahi wabihamdih (one hundred times daily)

'How perfect Allah is and I praise Him'

…a hundred times during the day, his sins are wiped away, even if they are like the foam of the sea'

(249)

Abu Hurayrah ﷺ reported that the Messenger of Allah ﷺ said: 'Whoever says at morning and evening time:

سُبْحَانَ اللهِ وَبِحَمْدِهِ (حين يصبح وحين يمسي)

Subhanallahi wabihamdih (at morning & evening time)

'How perfect Allah is and I praise Him'

…one hundred times, none shall come on the Day of Resurrection with anything better except someone who has said the same or even more'

morning: after prayer until the sunrises, **evening:** after asr prayer until the sunsets, however some scholars say: after the sunsets and onwards

(250)

Aboo Ayyub al-Ansari ؓ related that The Prophet ﷺ said: 'Whoever says:

لَا إِلهَ إِلَّا اللهُ وَحْدَهُ لَا شَرِيكَ لَهُ، لَهُ المُلْكُ وَلَهُ الحَمْدُ وَهُوَ عَلَى كُلِّ شَيْءٍ قَدِيرٌ

La ilaha illallahu wahdahu la sharika lah, lahulmulku walahulhamd, wahuwa 'ala kulli shay'in qadir

'None has the right to be worshipped except Allah, alone, without partener To Him belongs all sovereignty and praise and He is over all things omnipotent'

...ten times is like one who has freed four souls from among the children of Ismael'

(251)

Abo Hurayrah ؓ reported that the Messenger of Allah ﷺ said: '(There are) Two words, (which are) light on the tongue, heavy on the Scale and beloved to The Most Gracious:

سُبْحَانَ اللهِ وَبِحَمْدِهِ وسُبْحَانَ اللهِ العَظِيمِ

Subhanallahi wabihamdih, wasubhanallahil adhim

'How perfect Allah is and I praise Him How perfect Allah is, The Supreme'

(252)

Abo Hurayrah ﷺ reported that the Messenger of Allah ﷺ said: 'Saying:

سُبْحَانَ اللهِ، وَالحَمْدُ للهِ، لَا إِلَهَ إِلَّا اللهُ وَاللهُ أَكْبَرُ

Subhanallah, walhamdu lillah, la ilaha illallah wallahu akbar

'How perfect Allah is, and all praise is for Allah None has the right to be worshipped except Allah, and Allah is the greatest'
... is more beloved to me than everything the sun has risen over'

(253)

Sa'ad ﷺ said: 'We were sitting with the Messenger of Allah ﷺ, and he said: 'Are any of you unable to gain a thousand good deeds each day?' Somebody then asked him ﷺ: How does one achieve a thousand good deeds? He replied: 'He should say:

سُبْحَانَ اللهِ

Subhanallah

'How perfect Allah is'
...one hundred times, for a thousand good deeds are recorded for him or a thousand bad deeds are wiped away'

(254)

Jabbir related that the Prophet said:
'Whoever says:

سُبْحَانَ اللهِ العَظِيمِ وبِحَمْدِهِ

Subhanallahil 'adhimi wabihamdih

'How perfect Allah is The Supreme,
and I praise Him'

...a palm tree is planted for him in paradise'

(255)

'Abdullah Ibn Qays related that the Prophet said to him: 'O 'Abdullah Ibn Qays, shall I not inform you of a treasure from the treasures of paradise?' He then said: 'Say:

لَا حَوْلَ وَلَا قُوَّةَ إِلَّا بِاللهِ

La hawla wala quwwata illa billah

'There is no might nor power except with Allah'

(256)

'the most beloved words to Allah are four:

سُبْحَانَ اللهِ، والحَمْدُ للهِ، ولَا إِلَهَ إِلَّا اللهُ واللهُ أَكْبَرُ

Subhanallah, walhamdu lillah, wala ilaha illallah, wallahu akbar

'How perfect Allah is, all praise is for Allah None has the right to be worshipped except Allah and Allah is the greatest'

...it does not matter which of them you start with'

(257)

Sa'ad Ibn Abi Waqqas ؓ narrated that a man came to the Messenger of Allah ﷺ and said to him: 'Teach me something which I should say?' He said: 'Say:

لَا إِلهَ إِلَّا اللهُ وَحْدَهُ لَا شَرِيكَ لَهُ، اللهُ أَكْبَرُ كَبِيراً وَالْحَمْدُ لِلهِ كَثِيراً سُبْحَانَ اللهِ رَبِّ الْعَالَمِينَ، لَا حَوْلَ وَلَا قُوَّةَ إِلَّا بِاللهِ الْعَزِيزِ الْحَكِيمِ

La ilaha illallah, wahdahu la sharika lah, allahu akbaru kabira, walhamdu lillahi kathiran, subhanallahi rabbil alameen, la hawla wala quwwata illa billahil 'azizil hakim

'None has the right to be worshipped except Allah, alone without partener Allah is most great and much praise is for Allah How perfect Allah is, Lord of the worlds There is no might nor power except with Allah, The Exalted in might, The Wise'

...the man then said: 'These are for my Lord, and what is for me?' He ﷺ replied:

'Say:

اللَّهُمَّ اغْفِرْ لِي، وَارْحَمْنِي، وَاهْدِنِي، وَارْزُقْنِي

Allahummaghfir li, warhamni, wahdini, warzuqni

'O Allah, forgive me, have mercy upon me, guide me and grant me sustenance'

(258)

Tariq al-Ashja'i ؓ said: 'When someone would

embrace Islam, the Prophet ﷺ would teach him how to perform prayer and then order him to supplicate with the following words:

اللّهُمَّ اغْفِرْ لِي، وَارْحَمْنِي، واهْدِنِي، وعَافِنِي وارْزُقْنِي

Allahummaghfir li, warhamni, wahdini, w'afini warzuqni

'O Allah, forgive me, have mercy upon me, guide me, give me health and grant me sustenance'

(259)

Jabir Ibn 'Abdullah ؓ related that the Messenger of Allah ﷺ said: 'Verily, the best supplication is:

الْحَمْدُ لله

Alhamdu lillah

'All praise is for Allah'

…and indeed, the best form of remembrance is:

لَا إِلَهَ إِلَّا اللَّهُ

La ilaha illallah

'None has the right to be worshipped except Allah'

(260)

'The everlasting righteous deeds:

سُبْحَانَ اللهِ، والْحَمْدُ لله، لَا إِلَهَ إِلَّا اللهُ واللهُ أَكْبَرُ وَلَا حَوْلَ وَلَا قُوَّةَ إِلَّا بِاللهِ

Subhanallah, walhamdu lillah, la ilaha illallah, wallahu akbar, wala hawla wala quwwata illa billah

'How perfect Allah is, and all praise is for Allah None has the right to be worshipped except

Allah, and Allah is the greatest There is no might nor power except with Allah'

129. How the prophet ﷺ made tasbih

Tasbih, it means here, to say:
Subhanallah, alhamdu lillah, Allahu akbar

(261)
'Abdullah Ibn Amr ؓ said: 'I saw the prophet ﷺ make tasbih with his right hand'

O Allah, send peace and blessings upon our Prophet Muhammad, his companions, and his family and all those who follow them in righteousness till the Day of Reckoning
Amin

ALSO AVAILABLE FROM LIGHT PUBLISHING

www.ingramcontent.com/pod-product-compliance
Lightning Source LLC
Chambersburg PA
CBHW012005090526
44590CB00026B/3880